Contents

COPYRIGHT

WHEN ARE YOU A PROFESSIONAL?
- WHITHER GOEST?
- THE TRUE SPEAKER IS NOT A PERFORMING SEAL
- THE DIVERSE (AND DAUNTING) SPEAKER SCENARIOS
- THE VAGARIES OF THE TRADE
- SUMMARY

ESTABLISHING YOUR MARKET
- WHOM DO YOU WANT TO LISTEN?
- CREATING VALUE PROPOSITIONS
- STEPS TO CREATING MARKET "REACH"
- THE LITMUS TEST OF REAL, IMAGINARY, AND "WOO-WOO" MARKETS
- ORGANIZING YOUR APPROACH: THE EASIEST ROUTE IS USUALLY THE BEST
- SUMMARY

POSITIONING AND BECOMING AN OBJECT OF INTEREST
- TELL THEM WHAT THEY NEED TO KNOW, NOT EVERYTHING THAT YOU KNOW
- BEING AROUND A LONG TIME MAKES YOU OLDER, BUT NOT NECESSARILY BETTER
- TRANSFORMING INTELLECTUAL CAPITAL INTO INTELLECTUAL PROPERTY
- ESTABLISHING VIRAL INTEREST

- BEST PRACTICES TO INCREASE YOUR BUSINESS
- IF YOU DON'T BLOW YOUR OWN HORN, THERE IS NO MUSIC
- FISH SWIM, BUT DIFFERENT STROKES FOR DIFFERENT FOLKS
- SUMMARY

ESTABLISHING FEES
- HOW MUCH DO YOU CHARGE? HOW MUCH HAVE YOU GOT?
- THE THREE BASIC FEE RANGES YOU MUST CREATE
- TAKING OUT THE MIDDLEMEN: DEALING ONLY WITH TRUE BUYERS
- PROVIDING THE CHOICE OF "YESES"
- TURNING AN EVENT INTO A PROCESS AND TRIPLING YOUR SUCCESS
- 40 WAYS TO INCREASE YOUR FEES
- INCREASING FEE VELOCITY
- SUMMARY

MODERN MARKETING
- I DON'T CARE ABOUT THE COST
- THE MAGIC AND MYTH OF THE INTERNET
- WORKING (OR NOT) WITH BUREAUS AND AVOID BEING A HIRED HAND
- TRADE ASSOCIATIONS: MAKE MONEY AND MARKET CONCURRENTLY
- Tips to Leverage the Trade Association Marketplace
- WHERE AND HOW TO PUBLISH
- Some Other Comments
- How to Get a Book Published
- THE MARKET GRAVITY CYCLE
- SUMMARY

LEAN AND MEAN
- WEALTH IS DISCRETIONARY TIME
- Lean and Mean Speaking Practice
- ESSENTIAL AND LEGITIMATE STAFF CHARACTERISTICS
- SMALL PRINT: INCORPORATION, LEGAL, ACCOUNTING,

INSURANCE, TAXES, YADA
SUMMARY
DISCLAIMER

COPYRIGHT

Copyright © 2018 All rights reserved. No part of this book may be reproduced, stored in a retrieval system, or transmitted in any form or by any means, electronic, mechanical, photocopying, recording, scanning, or otherwise, without the prior written permission of the publisher.

WHEN ARE YOU A PROFESSIONAL?

WHITHER GOEST?

For a long time, if you told someone that you were a professional speaker, that person would immediately translate that into "motivational speaker," a phrase that represents everything that is wrong and empty-headed about this profession. Calling an excellent professional a "motivational speaker" is like calling dinner at a five-star restaurant a "meal," citing Willie Mays as an "outfielder," or calling Judy Garland a "singer."

Some phrases just don't do the subject justice.

Historically, professional speakers were evangelical, professional by dint of how they were trying to move the audience, as in Billy Sunday or Oral Roberts. There is a history of superb, moving, inspirational sermonizing and homilies in every religion. There have also been speakers whose intent was to enlighten the audience members about their own potential, not so much by offering pragmatic techniques as by offering stirring messages: "You can be your own best friend"; "You are the owner of the mortgage on your life!" Accompanied by experiences and exercises (taken over from early T-group and sensitivity training1), the speech morphed into workshops and "events."

In the 1960s we had Werner Erhart, and in the 1990s, Tony Robbins. In between and along the way, we've had thousands of pretenders to the motivational thrones. But these approaches were based largely on the personality of the originator, no less than the religious, charismatic speaker. (Very few Tony Robbins franchises have ever been successful, so far as I know. I used to mentor one such franchise owner. People wanted to see the master himself, understandably.)

Finally, we have "rallies," wherein an organizer fills an arena, often with the employees of a few companies that foot the bill, and marches out the likes of Colin Powell, George Bush, Zig Ziglar, and whoever else is on that circuit to "wow" the crowd. For a few hours people can hear some stirring commentary, buy some products (which will later gather dust on endless shelves), and return to work under the temporary belief that their company has just invested in their longterm well-being.2 (It's a lot cheaper than giving them raises or improved benefits.)

Those times have changed.

Oh, you'll still see a group of Goldman Sachs or Prudential senior managers out on some beach racing to build sand castles under the tutelage of an "energy coach" or a "motivation manager." But the only thing occurring there is sunburn.

Today, everyone had better be a motivational speaker, but there has to be steak to accompany that sizzle. That is, paying customers are expecting expertise in specific content areas presented in an engaging, provocative, and entertaining manner.

Thus, two extremes will not work:

1. Running around like the Mad Hatter trying to thrill people with vapid affirmations, such as, "They can heat you up, but they can't burn you!"

2. Standing rooted in the earth, talking through another boring PowerPoint presentation of 185 slides while people try to see their PDAs in the dark. (If you have enough iPhones, with screens aglow, in the audience during such a tedious presentation, it begins to resemble a silent rock concert.)

Here is why the market expectations and demands have

changed:

Increasingly sophisticated audiences. The mass media and the Internet have created a more intelligent expectation. People can readily watch experts on TED, for example (TED.com), and in 20 minutes (the time limit) be captivated by geysers on the ocean's bottom, synthetic happiness, urban planning, or modern communications devices.

Increasingly sophisticated buyers. Corporate executives and trade association directors demand a return on their investment. They don't need someone to "babysit" the audience for a few hours during a convention; they require topical expertise that can be utilized immediately in conjunction with organizational strategy and tactics.

An overabundance of schlock. There is no barrier—zero— to entry in the professional speaking market. A lot of people have sidled in, managed to get work, and flopped. Still more have decided to position themselves as commodities, charging very little in the hope of achieving for volume, and have done poor (and repetitive) work.

The economy contracted. Some lingering effects even during rebound and growth will be a more zealous analysis of external expenditures. Professional speakers have never exactly proved themselves to be irreplaceable or urgently needed. So the corporate zeitgeist has incorporated a "less is more" philosophy.

The association and (legitimate) connection with the training business. Most people who are making big money in speaking are doing so in training. (More on this later in the book.) Very few of us who are noncelebrity speakers can earn big money exclusively from keynoting, for example, and few of us want to, since the travel is ridiculous. However, training and human resources within corporations are increasingly discredited, so approaching through those routes is a rough road.

The profession is changing, but for the better. That's why it's easier than ever to build and sustain a thriving practice.

THE TRUE SPEAKER IS NOT A PERFORMING SEAL

This business is about intellectual firepower. Expertise can be defined as a thorough and encompassing knowledge of a particular subject matter, including its origins, application, strengths and weaknesses, future probabilities, and so forth. It's not about perfection or absolute wisdom, or even a personal repository of global information.

It's about helping others to improve in a given area. That improvement may be in the form of more knowledge, changed behavior, new standards, reduced stress, a more balanced lifestyle, more enduring relationships—whatever.

It's not about jumping through hoops, donning strange clothing, balancing blocks on your nose, juggling fireballs, or reading people's minds. All of the foregoing may be important at times and, if done well, certainly have entertainment value (well, not the juggling), but they are not what professional speakers focus on. Every gimmick you introduce dilutes your educational and developmental message. And there are myriad jugglers and ventriloquists.

But there are relatively few effective and engrossing professional speakers.

So unless you prefer to be paid in herring, here are some

Dr. Dennis Mulumba

parameters for your professional conduct and demeanor.

THE DIVERSE (AND DAUNTING) SPEAKER SCENARIOS

When I talk about "speaking" in this book, I'm embracing any and all of the following:

Keynotes. The keynote is literally the "key note" to a convention or conference and is properly the opening plenary session. When someone says, "I delivered the

closing keynote" or "I was one of the four keynoters," that person is a tad confused.

Plenary sessions. These are general sessions to which the entire conference is invited, and there can be only one or many. The keynote is always a plenary session. Plenary sessions can last from 20 minutes to 90 minutes, but are typically an hour.

Concurrent sessions. These are longer sessions that run simultaneously. Participants generally have their choices of which to attend, although they may be assigned based on need. These generally run from an hour to three hours, but are typically about 90 minutes.

Workshops and seminars. These are full-day and multiday programs. They may be within one organization or be "public sessions" that strangers are invited to attend. They are generally much more oriented toward skills transfer, practice, and application.

Generally, when you work for a large client, you are delivering sessions internally for that client. But when you are delivering public sessions, you are promoting these yourself and charging each individual attendee (although you may be subcontracted to do this by larger seminar training companies, which is like being in indentured servitude—at this writing, some are paying $300 per day).

Here are some variations of these roles:

After-dinner speakers. An after-dinner speaker is addressing a general session with a dozen or a thousand people to conclude an evening. It is one of the most difficult types of speaking in that the audience has usually experienced an open bar, a heavy dinner, wine with the meal, often an awards ceremony, some boisterous banter, and some droning talks by the top executives. It is not for the unconfident, inexperienced, or thin-skinned.

Humorists. These folks may appear anywhere on an agenda to lighten things up (if they're good) or poison things for everyone who follows (if they're not good). They often incorporate information about the organization and the people sponsoring the event into their humor. (Once again, we're not talking about celebrities such as Jay Leno or Jerry Seinfeld, although they'll do this kind of work if you pay them enough.)

Character portrayers. There are people who dress like Ben Franklin, Albert Einstein, Marilyn Monroe, Abraham Lincoln, or, presumably, Zorro who use the persona of their subject both to entertain the audience and to convey some pertinent points about personal and professional development. They frequently provide an exegesis of their subject's famous speeches or roles. These are novelty acts, tightly choreographed, that are often quite successful in schools as well as businesses.

Facilitators. Facilitators facilitate—that is, they are supposed to enable groups to communicate better, to resolve issues more expeditiously, and to deal with difficult issues in a collaborative, constructive manner. The best facilitators allow the groups to do most of the speaking, but they are often required to present summaries, demonstrate what's occurring, describe obstacles, and provoke debate.

Moderators. The moderator is typically the panel emcee who provides brief explanations of subjects and procedures, introduces the panelists, handles questions from the floor, and keeps the proceedings on time.

THE VAGARIES OF THE TRADE

The odds are that most of your college professors were deadly dull. That's because they were (and are) compensated for performing a task, which is to hold a class session and deliver information. If teaching is defined as imparting knowledge, few of them actually teach, since precious little knowledge is transferred and only a scintilla is retained, let alone utilized, after the examination.

Most speakers approach our profession in the same manner. They believe that they are being paid to deliver a speech. Nothing could be farther from the truth. Yet that is what most speakers convey in their interactions with the buyer, and that is what most of them cite in their fee schedules. Speaking has become a commodity business, with bureaus (and speakers themselves) providing hourly or daily rates for the presence of a body on stage. That's roughly the equivalent of a doctor who charges by the hour for performing open-heart surgery or an architect who charges by the size of the building. Plumbers, who do charge by the hour, do noble work, but it's much more difficult for me to ensure that my speaking pipes will hold water.

Speaking is a business that provides for the enhancement of the buyer's objectives in return for remuneration to the provider. So let's establish some definitions and parameters prior to delving into the rest of the book and its specific techniques.

The buyer is the person who signs the check or causes it to be signed. The buyer is rarely the meeting planner, although that is the person with whom some bureaus are most comfortable working, which is one of the weaknesses of that system. A buyer is not necessarily the CEO, although he or she may well be in smaller companies or in larger ones that are organizing a top-level meeting. The buyer is inevitably that person whose objectives are to be enhanced. He or she "owns" the outcome of the event.

Whether you are pursuing an organization or responding to a contact that the organization has initiated, try to find the buyer. If you can do so, you can connect your involvement to his or her desired business outcomes, thereby increasing not only your chances of obtaining the assignment, but also your ability to obtain higher fees.

Objectives are the results that are to be achieved through your participation. Delivering a keynote, speaking after dinner, facilitating a breakout group, and conducting two concurrent sessions are not results. They are tasks, and therefore they are commodities, subject to tough comparative shopping. This is why you'll hear a meeting planner so often say, "We've got $5,000 for this slot. Who can you get for us?" It's the height of absurdity. The real question is, "Here's what we want to achieve. What value do various alternatives provide so that we can make an intelligent ROI (return on investment) decision?"

Listen carefully. The mere act of helping to explore, understand, and clarify the buyer's objectives will add tremendous value to your contribution. That's why you should relentlessly pursue discussions with the buyer and submit your proposal directly to that person. Only the buyer has the volition and capacity to arrange for investments based upon return. (Meeting planners merely have budgets and have incentives to stay within those budgets, and they sacrifice quality for economy every day.) A key aspect of what consultants call "process consultation" is that a collaborative, diagnostic approach is itself intrinsically valuable.

The process you engage in is more valuable than your actual time on stage. The reason that the heart surgeon is so valuable is not the hours that it takes to remove diseased arteries. The value is in the 20 years of practice, the continuing study, the experiential base, and the superb judgment that enable the surgeon to perform such a delicate operation in those few hours. Doctors don't get paid by the blood vessel, and you shouldn't get paid by the adverb.

The process behind virtually any speech includes the following:

Initial talks with the client to determine the desired outcomes and your contribution to those outcomes

Often, additional conversations with intended audience members to determine their points of view and their challenges, and to develop some clientspecific examples

A study of the industry in general, the competition, and the client's role within that scenario

Design of the actual speech, which may consist of 50 percent standard points that you make, 25 percent specific client-centered material, and 25 percent audience exercises, interactions, new material, and so on

Discussion of your speech with the client and coordination with what precedes and follows you, as well as with any other speakers on the agenda6

Preparation of visuals, handouts, and/or performance aids

Practice

Actual delivery of the talk

Postsession follow-up with the client to determine what else may be necessary (e.g., another copy of some of the visuals), what the reactions were, how well the objectives were met, and so on

If you emphasize the process—and you may well have additional components—then the buyer can understand the comprehensive contribution you can make to his or her objectives. If you emphasize the 60 or 90 minutes, or even the full day, that you're on stage, then the buyer perceives that payment is due only for that relatively brief duration. You have the ability to educate the buyer, but you can't do that if you're not talking to the buyer and/or if you don't understand your own value in terms of that process.

SUMMARY

Professional speaking is a craft that revolves around the use of words to meet buyers' objectives. The outcome of a successful speech should be an overjoyed buyer, whose resultant testimonial is a paean to your skills. You manage and guide this process by focusing on the outcomes, understanding the overall value of the process that culminates in your time on stage, and dealing with people who make investment decisions based upon value delivered, not minutes spent. Professional actors aren't speakers. While it's important for you to be thoroughly prepared, it's sterile to be so tightly orchestrated that the audience perceives an off-the-shelf performance rather than an engaging interaction. People choose the plays and professional performances that they attend, but they usually have their speakers chosen for them. If you do a thorough job at the front end, understanding the audience and basing your value on the difference you can make in the members' personal and professional lives, then you'll be positioned to reap huge rewards. Ego-needs fulfillment, product sales, and adulation will follow as by-products. They should never be pursued as primary goals. When speakers appear primarily to meet their own needs, they are as obvious as a ham sandwich (emphasis on the ham).

Now that we have some common understanding of what professional speakers do and why, let's take a look at how to choose a market and why most speakers inexplicably foreclose options rather than expand them.

ESTABLISHING YOUR MARKET

WHOM DO YOU WANT TO LISTEN?

Speaking is about listening. Remember the tree falling in the deserted forest? If only the squirrels hear it, has it made a sound?

If you're speaking to an empty auditorium with only the service staff listening (or to a full house that is sound asleep or busy texting because you're totally irrelevant or insipid), are you speaking?

It's vital to determine two facts:

1. Who are the members of your audience? Whose actions and behaviors do you wish to improve?

2. Who are your buyers? Whose condition can you improve by appearing in front of those audiences?

Note: None of this is about YOU. It's about THEM. If they are not improved, you are not successful, no matter how many stories you tell, how much applause you receive, or the "good vibes" that you experience.

CREATING VALUE PROPOSITIONS

A value proposition is the point on your marketing arrow. It provides aerodynamics. (Too many speakers have a value elevator speech or pitch." It keeps you and the prospect focused. Here are its characteristics: it is

Brief

Output, not methodology, oriented

Broad enough to embrace many buyers

Brief (Did I mention that already?)

Some examples of poor and excellent value propositions are

P: I have a six-step sales process that I teach the audience.

E: I dramatically decrease sales closing time at less cost of acquisition.

P: I provide humor and entertainment throughout the conference.

E: I reduce stress and create superior learning environments.

P: I facilitate strategic retreats.

E: I help your senior team select optimal goals and create accountabilities to ensure that those goals are reached.

You get the idea. Your value is in the outcome, not the input.

It's about the new actions and behaviors that you can engender, and the improved condition for the buyer that they create. (Behind every professional and/or corporate goal is a personal goal. If I want you to improve teamwork, it means that I'm weary of acting as referee between the teams.)

You might have a single, generic value proposition. Mine is, "I improve individual and organizational performance." Now, that's pretty wide, right? But if someone says (as someone always does), "What does that mean?" or "How do you do that?" I reply, "I guess it is a tad vague, so why don't you give me a couple of examples of areas where you'd most love performance to be improved and I'll give you an idea of how I'd create a speech (or workshop or event) to do that."

The key is not to defend or explain, but to engage the buyer in the diagnostic. Let's both talk about how I can help you.

Some definitions:

Economic buyer. The person who can write a check or cause one to be produced by the computer. In a small business, it is usually the owner. In a large business, it is typically someone with P&L (profit and loss) accountability, a division or department head, and so forth. In Fortune 1000 companies, there are scores or even hundreds of economic buyers within the organization. In trade associations, the economic buyer is usually the executive director, and sometimes the program or education director.

Feasibility buyers. These are people who contribute to the decision to buy in terms of finance, culture, technology, trust, programming, or whatever. They can say no, but they can't say yes. They are often gatekeepers, barring the way. You must circumvent them or blast through them. Human resources people and training people are feasibility buyers 99 percent of the time.

Meeting and event buyers. Although these people are ostensibly in charge of creating and running an event, it is never their event. They are minions and organizers for the real economic buyer. Always ask, "Whose meeting is this? Who initiated it?" Although industry organizations such as the National Speakers Association place a premium on meeting planners and bureaus, these are people who are charged with conserving budget, not getting results. They will continually ask, "Can you do it for less? Can you do several things for one fee? Will you wash the windows?" You are wasting your time with these people.

Speakers' bureaus. These are middlemen dealing with middlemen. (Forgive the gender exclusivity, but "middle people" sounds like something from The Hobbit and Middle Earth.) They work with meeting planners. They take 25 to 35 percent of your fee, but they rarely market you effectively. In the past decade, they've had such a rough time that they've begun to charge the speakers and not the clients (for critiquing video demos, inclusion in catalogs, "showcases," special mailings, and so on). Anything you get from a bureau is gravy, but bureaus should not be a primary marketing focus. Later in this book, when I show you how to turn a speech into a process and quintuple your fees, you'll see why bureaus are like stegosauruses.

Thus: value proposition, audience, true buyer. Now, how do we approach them?

STEPS TO CREATING MARKET "REACH"

Here are the steps to defining your market scope—that is, how to determine the extent of your appeal to buyers. The wider the appeal to the more buyers, the better off you are. "Specialize or die" is nonsense.

1. Determine your value-added for the client. How are the buyer and the buyer's intended audience better off once you leave? A workshop, keynote, seminar, or "presentation" is merely a delivery vehicle. How are people actually improved?

Example: Your people will be able to identify a true buyer earlier and establish a peer relationship faster. For you (the buyer), it will mean far less time spent on corrective action and failure work.

2. Establish who your likely buyers are. In a larger organization, a buyer may have P&L responsibility or head a department or business unit. In a smaller operation, he or she may be the owner or CEO. In a trade association, the buyer may be the executive director or chair of the board.

Example: For the value proposition in point 1, your buyer would probably be the vice president of sales, the vice president of product management, or the owner of a medium-sized business.

3. Examine whether you should focus on particular markets. You may choose to stay within your general geographic area

Speaking Mastery

because of child-care needs, an aversion to travel, or a richness of local prospects. You may choose to focus on IT functions or manufacturing firms or financial services organizations because of your background and/or your affinity for them.

Example: You may focus on insurance sales because you began your career in insurance, you still have contacts there, and you are near the headquarters of large insurance companies.

4. Begin to create a body of work. Buyers are attracted to expertise. Start to write, speak, network, create blogs, record podcasts, conduct teleconferences, and so forth to build public examples of your expertise.

Example: Begin a newsletter on selling insurance services and products that you distribute electronically for free: The Insurance Assurance.5

5. Call everyone you know. Once you have begun to create a body of work that displays your expertise, contact everyone you can: family, friends, professional colleagues, suppliers, vendors, past clients, community acquaintances, and so on. Explain the value you are now providing, and ask if they—or anyone they know—can avail themselves of such value.

Example: Send an e-mail to all those people to whom you recommend others—doctors, dentists,

designers, accountants—so that they can reciprocate when appropriate.

6. Ensure that you are accessible. Make it easy for people to find you and do business with you. Have a quick and easy answering machine message and recording option. Allow people to send you e-mail via your Web site. Use a full signature file, including your physical address, in your e-mail. (If someone wants to hunt you down and kill you, that person really doesn't need to rely on finding your address in your e-mail.)

Example: Return all your calls within three hours, and all your e-mails within a day. Responsiveness is a key catalyst for new business.

7. Watch your language Speak in the buyer's language of results and outcomes.

Speaker Terms	Buyer Terms
❖ Conduct sales training ❖ Deliver the keynote ❖ Entertain after dinner ❖ Talk about stress reduction ❖ Deliver my message of hope ❖ Provide a motivational talk ❖ Convey time management skills ❖ Introduce quality techniques ❖ Instill a customer service attitude ❖ Describe my battle with illness ❖ Provide investment advice ❖ Teach interpersonal skills	❖ Improve sales closing rates ❖ Create a need to listen and learn ❖ Alleviate the day's stress, emphasize camaraderie ❖ Improve productivity ❖ Enable people to resolve their own Problems ❖ Challenge participants to exceed higher goals ❖ Improve productivity ❖ Reduce failure work that erodes Profitability ❖ Improve customer retention rates, cut attrition ❖ Broaden solution options for personal tragedy ❖ Maximize financial security ❖ Reduce conflict on

	the job

8. Learn the present and future "hot buttons." What are the current and short-term greatest needs of the markets and buyers that you've identified? How can you meet and exceed those needs? How can you go beyond just "fixing" (which is of moderate value) and find ways to raise the bar (which is of tremendous value)?

Example: How can senior management best organize, encourage, monitor, and reward a global sales force that it seldom sees, or telemarketing people who work from their homes?

9. Reach out through others. "Cold calling" doesn't work in this business, even though you'll hear people boast about calling someone out of the blue and obtaining business. (Do you buy investment securities from the people who call you at home at 8:30 at night?) But finding someone who knows someone who knows the buyer does work. Establish and treasure precious networks of lead sources.

Example: Someone in your club or church or soccer league works somewhere that is attractive for your plans. Ask if this person can introduce you to someone who knows someone who...

10. Plan for success, not failure. Too many professionals try to protect themselves against failure, but never plan to exploit success! Look for long-term potential in the markets that you examine and seek to penetrate.

Examples:

- ✓ Ability to sustain high fees within your value proposition
- ✓ Multiple booking potential (corporations with numerous sites)

- ✓ High-level audiences composed of potential buyers (trade associations)
- ✓ International potential for expansion (global organizations)
- ✓ Exposure in parts of the country where you haven't worked (travel is welcome)
- ✓ Ability to purchase added products or services (books, consulting)
- ✓ Potential for additional value propositions beyond the original
- ✓ Trend setters and early adopters in their industries or professions

11. Focus on process, not content. Processes (e.g., decision making, conflict resolution, sales techniques, influence, and so on) are applicable across industries and markets. You are always better off with that orientation than with a narrow one, such as "doctor/patient relationships in public hospitals."

Example: It's far too difficult to master content, but processes are easier. I've spoken on leadership and strategy for the National Fisheries Association, National Cattle and Feed Lot Association, American Radiological Association, Hewlett-Packard, and Bank of America. Only the examples were changed.

12. Go get bloodied. Some people make plans forever. Others go out, try, fail, learn pragmatically, and succeed the second or third time. Find some lower threat buyers at first (a small trade association, a medium-size business) and try some of this out. That's how you'll advance.

Example: Put all of this in your calendar and try it locally, at the very least. Find out what you're already good at and where you need more development. In the old Cheers television comedy, the bartender named Coach once told one of the leads, Diane, that he had been working on a book for six months. Diane was amazed and said, "I didn't know you were a writer."

"A writer?" asked Coach. "I've been trying to read it."

It doesn't take six months to read a book (or to write one). Even veterans procrastinate about that book they want to write, that tape series they want to record, and that radio show they want to host. This afternoon or this evening, start it. There's no one stopping you.

THE LITMUS TEST OF REAL, IMAGINARY, AND "WOO-WOO" MARKETS

You need three elements to speak successfully:

1. A market need that you identify, create, or anticipate

2. The competency to meet that need

3. Passion

If you have need and passion but no competency, someone else will always get the work. If you have competency and passion but no need, you have a message that no one wants to

Speaking Mastery

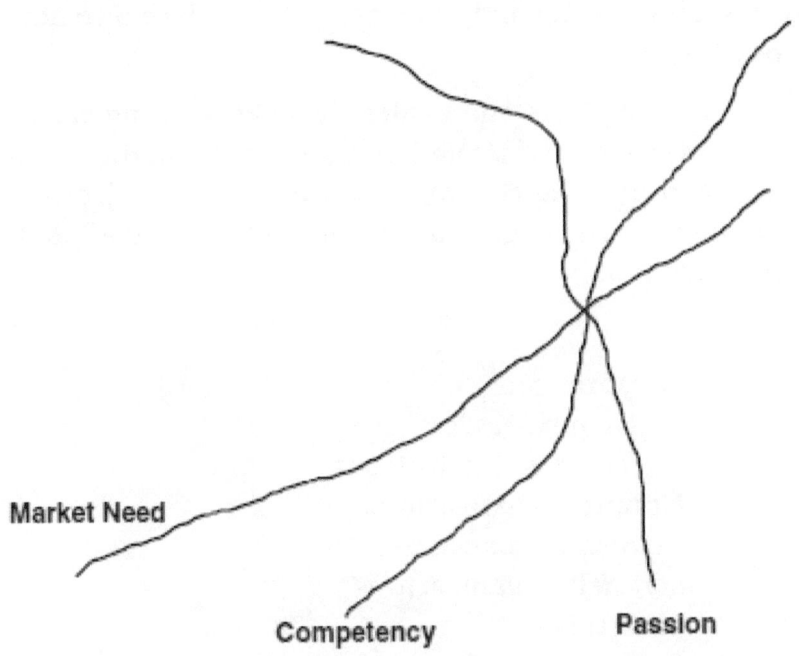

hear; and if you have need and competency but no passion, that's what I call a nine-to-five job.

There is preexisting need, such as areas of teamwork, strategy, sales, customer service, and so forth. There is need that you create, which might be using the Web to create electronic commerce. And then there is need that you anticipate, which might be having to manage people globally who are never together physically. (No one told Akio Morita at Sony that anyone wanted a device carried on the belt that played music through earphones. But the Walkman was a huge hit and the grandfather of the iPhone.)

Competency is the continuing self-development and creation of intellectual property that allows you to at least competently address client issues and, even better, raise the bar to new levels of performance.

Passion is the desire and resilience to keep going because you believe deeply in your ability to help the audience and the buyer, and because the job is so often about rejection. With these elements in place and correctly oriented, you can address markets such as

- ✓ Corporations
- ✓ Small businesses
- ✓ Educational institutions
- ✓ Nonprofit institutions
- ✓ Government agencies
- ✓ Self-help organizations
- ✓ Charities
- ✓ Public service firms
- ✓ Boards

If your expertise is a process, such as strategy or team building, then you can usually address many markets, since only the content changes. If your expertise is content, such as growing corn or conducting a census, then your markets are severely limited to those who are involved with such content.

Of course, in many instances, you may have expertise in both process and content. The greater your content knowledge (e.g., of the health industry) and your process expertise (compensation practices), the better the results you can generate (higher morale at cost-effective levels).

Content Knowledge	X	Process Skills	= Results
Decision making		Autos	Profit
Problem solving		Chemicals	Productivity

Negotiating	Insurance	Morale
Interviewing	Banking	Safety
Coaching	Electronics	Image

The litmus test for a legitimate market versus a "woowoo" market would include the following:

- ✓ Are there people already in this market (which indicates that there is value and the ability to pay—competition broadens markets)?
- ✓ Are there common needs spread over a critical mass of people?
- ✓ Can the buyer be clearly identified and accessed?
- ✓ Is the issue remediable and/or improvable?
- ✓ Do you possess the intellectual property, methodology, and approaches to address the topic?
- ✓ Is there sustainable business over time (is the population large enough)?
- ✓ Are people willing to pay, and will they be able to see improvement?
- ✓ Are the interests sincere and nonconflicting (we want you to improve morale while we lay off half the workforce)?
- ✓ Is the solution to the need such that speaking or training can be an effective intervention?

ORGANIZING YOUR APPROACH: THE EASIEST ROUTE IS USUALLY THE BEST

William of Occam formulated in the fourteenth century that the easiest route is usually the best, no matter what your goals. This has come down to us through the ensuing half-millennium as "Occam's razor." In my terms, too many people travel completely around the block just to arrive next door.

You want to reach true, economic buyers, and/or enable them to reach you. We've established that already. So what are your easiest routes?

First, start speaking. Wherever you can, within reason, take on speaking assignments. Speak at the local Rotary Club or facilitate a meeting of your Little League board of directors; moderate a panel at a town meeting; teach as a guest instructor at a community college. Don't go around the block. Knock on the doors next to you.

This kind of speaking has quite a few salutary effects:

- ✓ You can hone your skills through practice.
- ✓ You can try out new material.
- ✓ You can ask others for solicited feedback.

- ✓ You can record the sessions.8
- ✓ You can develop relationships with potential buyers and recommenders in the room.
- ✓ You can garner testimonial letters.9
- ✓ You can obtain referrals from the participants.
- ✓ You can send out a press release about the appearance.
- ✓ You may be interviewed or write an article for the organization's newsletter.
- ✓ You can invite potential buyers to see you.
- ✓ You can provide handouts giving your Web site, blog, products for sale, and so forth.
- ✓ You can assess the relevance and attraction of your topic and approach.
- ✓ You can network before and after the event.

I think you can see that, even if you're not paid a cent, there are diverse and attractive marketing advantages to simply getting out and speaking wherever you can where wise people gather.

At the outset of your career, don't limit the markets you pursue, because you want to maximize the opportunity to find buyers. Don't arbitrarily exclude any true buyer. The more adjectives you use in describing your value, the worse off and narrower you will be.

For example, "I help you accelerate sales closing time while reducing the cost of acquisition" is powerful and attractive to a wide array of buyers. But if you add to it,

"in the telemarketing, real estate investment field in New England," you've just switched from a trawler's net to a single fishing pole with a worm on the hook!

If you're engaging in the kind of marketing I'm recommending — speak wherever you can and allow buyers and recommenders to see you while you improve your craft—you'll be seriously expanding your opportunity to appeal to the broadest number of needs.

Dr. Dennis Mulumba

Once you've established a successful career, you should have the savvy and the experience to significantly broaden your appeal. Too many veterans fail to do this, but instead simply try to get better at what they're already quite good at. Moreover, the narrower your focus, the more the rug can be yanked from under you by more powerful brands (a wellknown author and speaker writes a new book on your subject), newer technologies (people are downloading, not buying, CDs today and may be doing something else entirely by the time you read this), loss of interest in the topic (diversity), changes in perception (wisdom of financial analysts), traumatic events (recessionary times), and obsolescence (Y2K). Organize your approach to the market so that it is broadly appealing, simple, and easy. Make William of Occam proud.

SUMMARY

The genesis of a successful speaking career is: "First, there was value."

Focus on how the client's condition will be improved as a result of your contributions (not merely "the speech"). Once you know that, you can both attract people to you and reach out to form relationships with them. But you must focus on real markets, not ones that you imagine or that someone claims to be pursuing at some professional chapter meeting. (I've often felt that most professional association annual conventions serve the purpose of members getting together to lie to each other about how well they're doing!) Keep it simple. William of Occam was right. Your market approach, your dealings with the client, and your delivery should be simple (though not simplistic). Great athletes have the capacity to make the most difficult positions, plays, and performance seem commonplace. We learn how difficult these things are only when we try them (which is why I was such a lousy shortstop).

Keep your focus on your value (how you can improve your clients' conditions), the true economic buyer (who can pay for that value), how you will pursue such buyers (outreach), and how they will be attracted to you (market gravity). That's how the best athletes play this particular game.

POSITIONING AND BECOMING AN OBJECT OF INTEREST

TELL THEM WHAT THEY NEED TO KNOW, NOT EVERYTHING THAT YOU KNOW

Buyers are drawn to expertise. That means that the smarts between your ears (your intellectual capital) must be manifest as a pragmatic means of improvement for others (intellectual property). The more you produce that unequivocally helps others over the long term, therefore, the more you are going to be sought by buyers. And when you're sought by buyers because they find your intellectual property to be of value, you do not have to spend long hours on building relationships, and fees are not important (value is important). Do I have your attention?

BEING AROUND A LONG TIME MAKES YOU OLDER, BUT NOT NECESSARILY BETTER

There is a tremendous debate among professional speakers as to how one should progress from part-time to full-time status. In fact, there are two deeply revered beliefs among veterans of the business, and like many deeply revered beliefs, they are egregiously false. As Oscar Wilde observed, a thing is not necessarily true just because someone dies for it.

- ✓ Deeply Revered Belief 1. You are not a professional—indeed, you haven't "made it" in the business—unless you are engaged in it full-time.
- ✓ Deeply Revered Belief 2. The longer you have been at it, the better you are.

My criterion for success is pleasing people who can write checks that clear the bank. Peer recognition—if it is based on merit and not on slobbering adulation—is wonderful, but it doesn't pay the mortgage, and it seldom impresses the buyer. Don't tell me about the industry awards you've garnered and the strange initials after your name. Tell me about how you'll improve my business.

Speaking Mastery

We'll discuss fees in the next chapter, but while we're on the subject of the "full-time fallacy," let's debunk one more piece of horrid advice. There's an industry rubric that states that you should raise your fees when demand exceeds supply. That's roughly akin to saying that you should swim away from the beach until you can see land again. There's an awful lot of water out there.

And there's an awful lot of time in a year. In this case, is supply 5 days a week? Actually, you might be able to speak twice a day, and even on weekends. Maybe supply is 700 speeches a year? Supply and demand are commodity measures. They are not measures of value. Raise your fees— no matter how many times a year you speak—when your value to the buyer increases. And never forget that wealth is discretionary time; money is merely fuel. A lot of speakers work so hard earning money that they erode their wealth (never see their families or engage in leisure activities).

If full-time/part-time isn't the indicator of speaking success, does that mean that one can (shudder) work at another job and also be a speaker? Of course it does. Let's take the most extreme case. Suppose you're holding down a conventional 40-hour, nine-to-five career. However, you've managed to secure local speaking opportunities in the evenings and on weekends (or during vacations). If you're paid for them, you're a professional speaker, and you might be quite happy with the arrangement.

The definition of professionalism isn't your lifestyle or how you choose to spend your time. The point is whether you earn money for working on the platform. I know a dental hygienist named Denise who is married with children. She works full-time in her field. She also addresses dental groups, medical offices, conventions, and trade associations as her schedule permits. She's funny, effective, and highly regarded. She chooses her assignments based upon the demands of her professional schedule and her family's needs. Denise is an excellent professional speaker, a fine dental hygienist, a wonderful mother and wife ... well, do you get my drift?

Too many speakers waste too much time trying to determine how to leave their present occupations and/or reduce their other time commitments so that they can spend more time on professional speaking as if that were an end in itself. If speaking is to be your total calling, you'll naturally gravitate there because the gratification, job offers, and involvement will result in that evolution. But you can't force it.

People who pursue other interests or have additional careers (which I do, as a consultant, and Denise does, as a hygienist) are also speakers. They are not poor stepcousins of professional speakers; they are professional speakers, no less than someone who tries to speak every day and travels 95 percent of the time.

Fish swim. Speakers speak. No one challenges a fish at rest with, "I see you're not swimming, so for the moment we're not going to accept you as a fish."

Don't be awed by the size and scope of this industry. There are people who have been embraced by the bureaus, who have the connections, and who are most visible at industry conventions. But many of the newcomers I've seen are a lot better than the veterans who seem to rely on name recognition and a hackneyed "act" rather than trying to meet the business challenges of their contemporary customers.

There are approximately 10,000 or so trade associations, labor unions, professional societies, and technical groups that hold conferences each year, and many of them hold dozens of conferences annually.2 If we add over 120,000 businesses in the nation and their conferences and meetings, even eliminating those that have no need for external resources, we can realistically assume there are in excess of 100,000 meetings a year utilizing professional speakers. (After all, 2,000 per week is only 40 per state, or eight per state each day; there are probably hundreds every day in New York City alone.)

The meeting "industry" is in need of new talent. No executive investing in a meeting wants to present the "same old, same old." Don't make the mistake of assuming that you have to earn your merit badges through long apprenticeships and careful climbs to the top. If you want to climb the mountain, fine, but there are choppers available. One of the worst fates for an actor is to be typecast, which means that people can credibly accept that actor only in a type of role that he or she has been identified with before. That's a career-limiting dynamic. Some can escape this fate— Tom Hanks went on to diverse, award-winning roles after starring in a vacuous television sitcom. But Shelly Long has had a much tougher time post-Cheers. The jury is still out on James Gandolfini post-Sopranos. Similarly, veterans in the profession have often stumbled into a success trap, in which they were able to establish a niche but then fell victim to it. Speakers shouldn't be typecast either. If you're relatively new to the business, you have the advantage of being lighter on your feet and more versatile.

So disregard both of the deeply revered beliefs that we began with. It doesn't matter how many speeches you make a year, and it doesn't matter how long you've been in the business. All that matters is that buyers hire you, you meet their objectives, and you're paid for doing so. The degree and amount are up to you. But I know of no full-time speakers.

TRANSFORMING INTELLECTUAL CAPITAL INTO INTELLECTUAL PROPERTY

If speakers are sought because of their expertise, then it's fairly important that you make your expertise manifest. That is, no one really knows what's between your ears—and often, that includes you!

Just as we (incorrectly) expect that our prospects will appreciate our abilities, wit, and singing quality as much as our clients who know us well, we often assume that our prospects somehow, magically, can immediately sense all of our distinguishing assets and strengths.

That doesn't happen. Consequently, you have to transform what's in your head to what's on the table. (If there's not much going on inside your head, then thus far in this book you've probably been looking only at the pictures.)

Intellectual property is a marketing tool as much as a delivery mechanism. Here are just a few examples, from the ridiculous to the sublime:

Books	Booklets	Position papers
Teleconferences	Podcasts	Video clips
Chat rooms	Manuals	Tip sheets
Conversation	Visual aids	Handouts
Workshops	Web site	Blog
Articles	Newsletters	Reference materials
Downloads	CDs	DVDs

You get the idea. The things you say, depict, explain, represent, and so forth are tangible expressions of your intellectual property. It's never too soon or too late to improve and expand on these. You can protect them through trademarks, service marks, registration, and copyrights, which we'll talk about later. You can find my intellectual property expressed in every single medium I've listed.

To create intellectual property, such as that described in the preceding lists, proceed through this sequence:

1. How can I help people improve (their performance, self-worth, productivity, leadership, strategy, teamwork, and so forth)?

2. What specific ideas (models, approaches, techniques, methodology) do I or can I provide to create that improvement?

3. What forms best convey those ideas (print, audio, video, experiential, periodic, interactive)?

4. Are these forms best used for marketing, delivery, or both?

Here's an example. Let's say that you improve teamwork by changing what is normally a committee structure, with competing interests, to a true self-directed group that "wins or loses" together.

Let's decide that you can write an article for the trade press on the differences between a true team and a committee, you can create a checklist to audit the structures in your organization for marketing purposes, you can produce a keynote highlighting the differences and why they are crucial to performance, and you can design a workshop to transfer the skills.

Voila! You now have two free marketing devices and two highly lucrative delivery mechanisms. It's that easy. Some caveats: make sure that you use solely your own intellectual property, and that anything you "borrow" you have permission to use and you duly attribute it. This is important not only for ethical reasons, but also for pragmatic ones: too many speakers use secondary sources (other speakers) and focus on patently false information. (The Chevrolet Nova didn't sell in Mexico because "no va" means "no go" in Spanish.) Also, there are too many of the same stories going around ("When I was watching the electric parade in Disneyland . . . " or "A boy found a sand dollar on the beach . . ."). Please.

For the record, anything you write that is originally yours is automatically copyrighted in your name. You may add, as most of us do, # Dr. Dennis 2019 or Copyright Dr. Dennis 2019 (you don't need both the word and the symbol). The only reason to file with the commissioner of patents and copyrights—which is tedious, given all that we produce—is that if you ever sue someone for infringement, you can't collect punitive damages if you haven't thus filed. I've never bothered, but talk to your own trademark and copyright attorney to see what's in your best interests.

A trademark (TM) and a service mark (SM) refer to protection for phrases, models, materials, techniques, and so forth. The registration mark (1) indicates that the protection is finalized after a period of 6 to 12 months without challenge. Do not use Web-based software to save money when you try to trademark your work. Use a good attorney who specializes in the field, not your uncle's cousin Louie. The cost is almost always less than $1,000. (And you'd be surprised at the law. You can't, for example, protect a book title.)

Produce and protect your intellectual property. No one else is going to do it for you.

ESTABLISHING VIRAL INTEREST

These days it's easier than ever to create viral interest in your work. By this I mean that it's highly productive to get people talking, but not always in the manner you think.

First, let me debunk social media platforms as effective viral marketing tools for speakers. (I told you, intellectual property is about causing controversy!)

This is an unscientific, undocumented, and probably unpopular analysis of what I'm learning as King of Social Media. (I'm reminded of a great review of a leading actor in King Lear by Eugene Field: "He played the king as though under momentary apprehension that someone else was about to play the ace.")

Here are my anecdotal observations.

If people visit LinkedIn twice a day for 15 minutes each time, that's 2.5 hours in a five-day week. (I'm discounting weekends, although I shouldn't, because social media wandering is clearly a full-time avocation, but I want to be conservative here.)

If they visit Facebook four times a day for 10 minutes each, that's roughly 3.3 hours.

If they Twitter six times a day for five minutes each time, that's 2.5 hours. (Or 12 times at 2.5 minutes each—you get the idea.)

If they post on their blogs three times a week (it's rather important to keep a blog active and interesting), and if the creation and posting of the item takes 30 minutes (and I think I'm really lowballing this one), that's 2.5 hours. (Blogging can be very useful in moderation.)

And now I'm going to add just two hours to the week to accommodate reading others' blogs, replying to commentary, following up social media stuff offline, updating profiles, uploading photos, and so on.

Drum roll, please: during a five-day week on a conventional 40-hour basis, we now have about 13 hours used to engage in what are somewhat inappropriately termed "social media." I understand that those hours may well extend into evening or early morning time. On the basis of a 40-hour week, that's 33 percent devoted to this stuff, but even on the basis of a 12-hour day, the percentage is 22 percent.

If you were to devote less than half of those 13 hours, say 6 hours, to other professional marketing pursuits, I estimate that you could do any one of the following during that week:

- ✓ Write two or three chapters in a book.
- ✓ Create 10 to 12 position papers and post them on your Web site.
- ✓ Call, at a moderate pace with follow-up, 30 past clients and/or warm leads.
- ✓ Send out a dozen press releases.
- ✓ Engage in a full day of self-development or a workshop.
- ✓ Create three speeches or a complete multiday workshop.
- ✓ Create a new product to be sold on your Web site.
- ✓ Create, and develop a marketing plan for, a teleconference.
- ✓ Create and record three podcasts.
- ✓ Create and tape a video.
- ✓ Contact 30 prior clients for testimonials, referrals, or references.

- ✓ Attend two networking events.
- ✓ Create and distribute two newsletters.
- ✓ Complete at least half of a professional book proposal for an agent.
- ✓ Respond to 50 or more reporters' inquiries on, say, PRLeads.com.
- ✓ Seek out two high-potential pro bono opportunities.
- ✓ Contact and follow up with five trade associations for speaking opportunities.

And over the course of a couple of months, you can easily do ALL of the bullet points if you have a mind to do so. I'm allocating six hours a week, just over an hour a day.

My current evaluation is this: don't confuse occupation with avocation. I've never said that social media are evil or that they will not help someone find a buyer somewhere at some time. Heck, I've become an avid blogger, and I visit Facebook and Twitter daily. Yet I can still do all of the bullet points listed earlier and work only 20 hours a week.

If you're serious about corporate consulting and coaching, and my blog IS located at contrarianconsulting.com, then I'll continue to advise you that you're not going to find those buyers on social platforms. Is it impossible? No. Have some people done it? They claim so. But if you're engaged in social browsing at the EXPENSE of those bullet points, then that's not a good disposition or apportionment of your time. If you can do both, and still live a balanced and fulfilling life by your terms, then go for it.

BEST PRACTICES TO INCREASE YOUR BUSINESS

Here, then, is a brief discussion of nine best practices for the novice or the established speaker who wants to increase business dramatically and take an easier way to the top of the mountain.

1. Never Respond to the Question, "What Do You Speak About?"

Your orientation should always be on what you accomplish for the client. Don't focus on what you do; focus on how the customer benefits. Don't talk about why you're good; talk about what the buyer needs. Above all, don't prematurely and arbitrarily narrow your appeal, which a "topic list" will invariably do.

2. Prepare Well, but Not Fanatically

It's as important not to be perfect as it is to be well prepared. No speech that you or I will ever make will mark the turning point of modern civilization. With luck, your speeches might mean a bit of improvement in a person's professional and/or personal life. The difference—to the customer—between your being 90 percent prepared and 100 percent prepared (whatever that is) is infinitesimal. It is not perceived. But the energy expended in moving from 90 percent to 100 percent is immense, much more than that required to move from 75 percent to 95 percent.

Heresy? I know. But it's time we took apart the fantasy of perfection in this business, along with its attendant fanatical preparation. We are not building the space shuttle. We're not even trying to build a Toyota. There's just no need for frenzied anticipation. At 90 percent, your slides are rehearsed and placed correctly, you have a backup plan if the projector fails, your examples have been adjusted for the audience, and you can alter your timing given the progress of those before you. Enough.

One of the best ways to prepare is to record your speech a week or so earlier and then listen to it a few times. Practice some current humor to throw in each time, think about how you'll manage the visual aids during each segment, and work on making smooth transitions. When you're tired of listening to it, you're done practicing.

3. Adhere to Basic Adult Learning Needs

There are those who will tell you that there is a formula to a speech: you open with a humorous story, make a point, tell an anecdote, repeat your point, and close with a deeply personal revelation. That might help you deliver a speech in a choreographed manner, but I think you can see it coming a mile away.

Adult learning generally occurs in the sequence depicted in. This sequence shouldn't be a lockstep formula, but it does reflect what we know about human learning. We are presented with potentially useful information, practice with it to explore its utility, receive feedback on our use or performance, and then apply it in real life. Without the final step, all else is academic.

The discussion aspect can include humor, audience participation, and a host of other devices. It needn't be simply a "talking head" (although that's what it usually was in school). The practice element can include exercises, role-plays, games, and simulations, or it can be as simple as focusing someone on how a concept might be applied. The feedback constitutes the need to provide insights for the practice, and it can be selffeedback, feedback from colleagues, or feedback from the

Discussion	Practice	Feedback	Application
Lecture	alone	oneself	immediate
interaction	in teams	partner	delayed
demonstration	mentally	speaker	independent
example	in writing	delayed	with others

speaker. Application means that the audience has done something more than merely sit through your presentation.

These steps apply more to a workshop than to a keynote, but they have applicability for all adult learning. Even in a brief keynote, you want to present ideas and instill action in the participants. (This is why keynotes require different skills and can sometimes be more difficult to craft than much longer presentations.)

4. Understand Your Role as a "Motivational Speaker"

There is a difference between motivation and inspiration. To be inspired is to be spiritually moved, emotionally involved, and uplifted, and to take solace in words themselves. Its derivation is from theology. There's nothing wrong with being inspired, but it's usually a temporary, euphoric feeling, not a long-term focus on action.

Motivation is intrinsic. It comes from within. It is a willingness to act based upon a belief that the actions are important and will be gratifying. I cannot motivate you; you can only motivate yourself. However, I might be able to help establish an environment and atmosphere that are conducive to your becoming motivated. (Which is why motivation in the workplace is most directly a function of the immediate leadership and environment. It's plain silly to have a speaker try to motivate an audience that will then be returning to a gulag.)

Every good speaker is a motivational speaker because he or she helps people to take action. Motivation and self-esteem are intertwined, and self-esteem is heightened when someone receives tangible skills that, when used, will add to the person's success, encouraging him or her to apply those skills repeatedly. In essence, the more successful I am, the better I feel about myself, and the better I feel about myself, the more successful I am. But that's a tautology. The key to influencing that circle is to provide discrete skills that I can rely on for success.

To the extent that we impart those skills to others, we are all motivational speakers. I've never known how to reply when someone asks, "Well, are you one of those 'motivational' speakers?" I guess I'd better be.

Motivational speaking has developed a bad name because it's sometimes delivered as an empty, quasi-inspirational talk filled with platitudes, bromides, and the bathos of personal struggles, delivered by an empty suit. "You can't take away my best friend, myself," and "You can knock me, but you can't reach me" are cute phrases, but they are hard to apply in

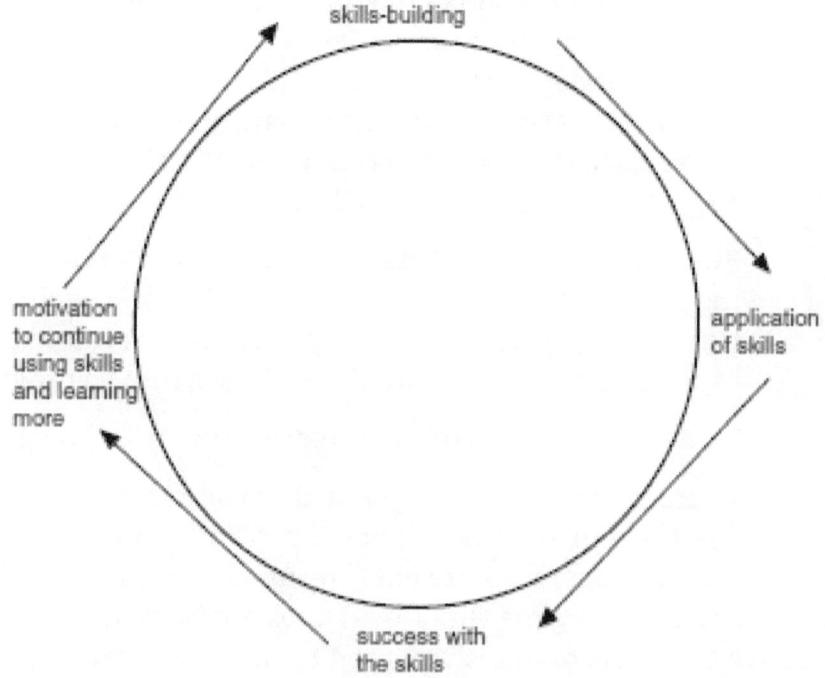

The Motivation Circle

the workplace the next day. On the other hand, learning a technique to resolve conflict with a coworker or learning how to influence the boss's delegation style can help me tangibly and immediately.

What's more motivational: being told that I'm my own best friend or being able to eliminate some of the stress in my life?

5. Self-Disclose Only if You Have a Point

Among professional speakers, the personal revelations known as self-disclosure have moved from a minor technique to the main attraction. When we involve ourselves and our experiences on the platform, we've too often moved from modest litotes to egocentric hyperbole. Here's a satire I use with my mentees to make the point:

> The astronaut had traveled to the moon with only a tenth of an inch of metal between him and the void. He had landed a quarter of a million miles away and walked tentatively but triumphantly on the cratered surface. Now, he was to return home in the final, tiny stage of rocket that awaited him.
>
> But something went terribly wrong. Instead of heading for Earth, he tumbled out of control in the direction of deep space. All attempts to correct his errant capsule failed, and he sailed, helplessly, into the abyss.
>
> Ladies and gentlemen, I am that astronaut...

Self-disclosure works if there's a point that the audience members can use to improve their condition. Telling me that you were born poor and now you're not (presumably because you're making money telling me this story) does not help me unless I can relate to the techniques you used to make that transition. Sharing your heartbreak, disease, loss, or vicissitudes with me may help you unburden yourself weekly, but it doesn't help me unless I can translate it to my condition and my life.

Some "experts" actually claim that the speaker's relationship with the audience is a function of the audience's need for help and the speaker's need for approval. That sounds like a bad case of codependency to me. I believe that the speaker-audience relationship is based upon shared values (we'd like to improve), trust (the speaker is factual), pragmatism (these are useful techniques), and relevance (this applies to us). If, as a speaker, you need approval, see a therapist.

6. Have Something to Say before You Write, Then Write Often

Don't use secondary sources because they're often actually farther removed than that and can be highly misleading. Find your own sources. More important, form your own opinions.

Look around in awareness and digest what you see. Are people more stressed when they work at home? Are decisions actually of poorer quality when they are made participatively? Does most training accomplish next to nothing six months later?

Don't be afraid to be contrarian, but be scared out of your mind to be trite. It's better to stand out in a crowd through controversy than to blend into the wallpaper through blandness. Your favorite color shouldn't be plaid. Writing will enable you to express your thoughts, examine your cognitive processes, and anneal your concepts. It doesn't matter whether you get published, although your odds are strikingly higher if you have written something as compared to having written nothing. Writing and speaking are synergistic and symbiotic. John Updike once explained that to understand how people speak—to be able to write dialogue—you have to understand how they think. I believe that to speak to people, you have to understand how you think.

7. Develop and Use Only Personal Anecdotes and Stories

Everyone is sick to death of the boy who throws the sand dollar back into the ocean.4 The naval ship that keeps requesting the lighthouse keeper to move to avoid a collision is about as old. These stories were poignant and funny once. So were silent films.

All around our personal lives revolve stories, incidents, circumstances, and travails of family, friends, and strangers. Jot them down, record them on tape, or create reminders for yourself (I keep an "anecdote file"). Go through them periodically to select those that have the potential to prove a point or highlight a concept. Feel free to embellish—after all, it's your story, and the key is the audience's improved condition, not personal historical veracity.

Never discard an anecdote. Even those that seem to hold no

promise may emerge as brilliant departure points as you mature, your speeches evolve, your clients change, and society diversifies. In the worst case, the anecdote takes up some space, but if you discard it, you lose it forever.

Personal stories immunize you from being copied and keep you unique no matter who else is on an agenda. No one can tell your stories as well as you can, and no one has your personal history and experiences. Collect and nurture the stories of your life. They are your continually renewing resource.

IF YOU DON'T BLOW YOUR OWN HORN, THERE IS NO MUSIC

This section of the chapter is for those of you who are relatively new to the profession or who seem to be stalled at a low level of activity. Once you're moving with some headway, it's relatively easy to change direction. But as long as you're becalmed, you're helpless to follow a course.

There are many options available to create your own power. They include

- ✓ Working for a seminar training firm
- ✓ Obtaining sponsorship
- ✓ Securing another speaker's cast-off business
- ✓ Volunteering your services in return for exposure
- ✓ Broadening your scope
- ✓ Serving as a backup

Working for a Seminar Training Firm

These firms include organizations such as Vistage and Fred Pryor Seminars. Quite a few very successful speakers began with these companies. They offer very inexpensive seminars (typically $39 to $99) and/or meetings for owners of small firms, for a limited duration, around the country, drawing from a cadre of speakers and trainers who make up the "faculty."

The true seminar companies either create or purchase their course content independently; the instructor doesn't need to bring his or her own material (in fact, they prefer that you don't). You learn the content, practice teaching with a veteran, and you're off and running. You'll be asked to commit to a basic number of days—say, 10 per month—in return for that guarantee from the company. The pay is dreadfully low, generally about $300 per program at this writing, although there are some exceptions for high performers and commissions on book and tape sales. (The firms that organize "management meetings" often forbid you to market to the participants!

The advantages include exposure all over the country, accolades for your press kit experience dealing with diverse audiences, a guaranteed cash flow, learning new concepts (you can teach several different programs), and at least half of your time free to market yourself as a professional speaker.

The disadvantages include a demand on half your time (reducing your flexibility), considerable travel (which is part of our business anyway, however), very low pay, constraints on what you can and can't do in the seminars, and continual monitoring—these firms are paranoid about instructors developing their own prospects during the courses, and with good reason.

All things considered, these arrangements are quite helpful if you see them as temporary bridges to the next step in your career growth. As a permanent job, they're roughly equivalent to the rowers in the Roman galleys. No matter how hard you work or how well you row, they're going to kill you.

Obtaining Sponsorship

Some organizations will pay a speaker to appear on their behalf. For example, Apple Computer might hire someone to address school groups on the best uses of technology in the classroom, a communications company might hire someone to address police and fire departments about crisis management, or a health maintenance organization might employ someone to address community groups on the benefits of early screenings for certain illnesses.

These are not sales pitches. They are informative presentations whose sponsors want to increase their profile, goodwill, and long-term business through their support of such efforts. Utilizing a professional speaker rather than a company spokesperson creates much less of a sales environment and much more of a professional presentation.

The advantages include guaranteed work, exposure, the ability to use your own concepts and techniques in support of your sponsor's needs (the sponsor might ask you to help design the session), and a firm client to cite. Depending on the nature of the organization, the pay could be menial or meaningful. The disadvantages include a probable lack of buyers for your future speaking in your audiences and the potential of being cast in a narrow niche (she's a health-care specialist).

Sponsorships virtually never seek you out. Your best bet is to find a firm that is using such tactics (or that could benefit if it did) and present your case to the buyer. Relatively few people do this aggressively, and you could have their undivided attention if you make a strong case, again, toward their objectives.

Dr. Dennis Mulumba

Securing Another Speaker's Cast-Off Business

All of us who have arrived at certain levels of success receive inquiries about business that we don't want to pursue. This is usually because the client can't afford the fee, it's in an area in which we're not sufficiently relevant, it calls for travel that isn't attractive, and/or it conflicts with other professional or personal activities. It happens to me at least several times a year, so it's happening out there every day as you read this.

Reach out to speakers who are in this situation. I don't mean that you should call them once a week and ask for a handout, because that's what it would be if there's no quid pro quo. Develop a relationship as you would with a client, bureau, or banker. Can you do some research for the speaker in return for the first call on appropriate business that he or she can't handle? Does the speaker need some office help, some temporary staffing, some computer work? Can you walk the dog and wash the car? (All right, I'm kidding, but not by much.)

Establish that kind of relationship with three or four busy speakers, and you might get their castoffs on a regular basis. If you're good, you'll be able to address the topic and earn credibility with the audience (which won't always be the case in these situations). Your fee will be no problem, since you'll be a bargain compared to the original, and you'll probably receive a higher fee than you would if you had been contacted directly.

The advantages are in the association with proven pros, the ability to work with firms that otherwise would never have called, and the opportunity to "test the envelope" in terms of your versatility and appeal. There are few disadvantages if you are able to establish a truly trusting relationship, and you're not simply around for legwork and as a "hanger on."

Volunteering Your Services in Return for Exposure

Every service organization, community group, social club, youth group, and local professional society can use speakers, especially if they're for free! The key to volunteering for these roles is that you want to do it for groups that will have potential customers in the audience. The ironclad rule for addressing these groups is simple: always bring a lot of business cards and handout collateral.

The Rotary, for example, typically has both owners of small businesses and managers from larger organizations, as well as community leaders. Civic organizations will have, by design, top people from large businesses on their boards and committees (e.g., the Greater Peoria Business Improvement Coalition). Occasionally, these entities will pay at least an honorarium. But it's more important to achieve the exposure to the people in the group than it is to make small change.

FISH SWIM, BUT DIFFERENT STROKES FOR DIFFERENT FOLKS

There is no single way to make it in this business. Bertrand Russell once said, "Don't ever be absolutely sure of anything—not even if I tell you."

Professional speakers help people and organizations improve their condition. They do it in a wide variety of ways, employing a vast array of talents. You have to decide what your "playing field" is and what kinds of plays make sense once you're on it. Ignore the stentorian, dire pronouncements

of those who, with fingers pointed skyward, proclaim that you must specialize, you must speak only for a fee, you must speak full-time, you must work with bureaus, you must have a demo video, you must eat bran every day.

The only "must" is to be flexible and not rule out options that may be useful to you as you advance your career. And we are all trying to advance our careers every day, newcomer and veteran, high profile or low. Some of us are simply less part-time than others.

Observe what people whom you respect have done. (Don't just

listen to advice because it's too easy to give it.) And watch a wide variety of people. Adapt those techniques that seem most relevant to you, and perhaps a few that will help you to stretch. Through this exploration, you can determine your true value to the client, and that will help you establish your fees, commensurate with that value.

SUMMARY

"Thought leadership" is the latest trendy phrase to describe an immutable condition: people are drawn to objects of interest, to expertise, and to power. No matter where you are in your career, you have the ability to create this kind of repute.

One primary requisite is to be concise. Tell people what they need to know, not everything that you know. You are a professional speaker in business environments, not a raconteur in a salon. A speaker who tells the same tired stories and uses shopworn examples year after year may land some jobs, but he or she won't build a career.

Your greatest asset is between your ears: intellectual capital. You must instantiate this so that it is manifest as intellectual property. IP takes many forms, speaking merely being one (and most speeches aren't immediately copyrighted unless you provide some written transcription, which is rare).

You can increase your business in diverse ways, and you should follow the best practices for doing this, not attempt to reinvent cold beer. That increase will add to your reputation as a thought leader, which enhances viral marketing and mention. In this technological age, that is easier than ever, though not on some of the most touted platforms (social media).

At the end of the day, however, if you haven't blown your own horn, there probably hasn't been much music.

ESTABLISHING FEES

HOW MUCH DO YOU CHARGE? HOW MUCH HAVE YOU GOT?

FOR those of you who turned immediately to this chapter upon opening the book, my warmest welcome. When you get the chance, you may want to visit the preceding chapters. Professional speaking is a business. What you make is far less important than what you keep.

THE THREE BASIC FEE RANGES YOU MUST CREATE

Nobody is worth all that much by the hour. My auto mechanic makes about $125 per hour for his shop, some speakers command $7,500 for a keynote, and Colin Powell, the former chairman of the Joint Chiefs of Staff, commands about $75,000 for an hour appearance at a convention. That's 10 times the average keynoter fee and 600 times the mechanic's rate. How can this be? Does Colin Powell have 10 times or 600 times their life experiences, skills, preparation, intelligence, and abilities?

The fact, of course, is that the hour (or half day or day) that we spend on the platform is not the value of what any of us brings to the client, yet we insist on charging fees for that time commodity, rather than for our true value. In reality, the mechanic is able to charge $125 an hour because of the experience, training, expertise, and talents that enable him or her to fix your car, provide the proper preventive maintenance, and ensure that the proper performance endures long after you're out of the shop. That same process applies to you, me, and Colin Powell as well.

People in the audience come to hear an hour keynote,1 but the buyer is paying you to deliver it because of some combination of the following factors. I call it the "value list" because it represents those aspects of what you do that the buyer finds of worth.

Value List for Speakers

- ✓ Your repute in the field
- ✓ The talents you bring to bear in delivering each speech
- ✓ Your singular knowledge or approaches
- ✓ Your particular platform skills
- ✓ The visual aids or demonstrations that you provide
- ✓ Your ability to speak to that particular industry
- ✓ The skills that you'll impart to the audience
- ✓ Your experiences, stories, anecdotes, and/or humor
- ✓ The behavior change that will ensue
- ✓ The improvement in the business that will result
- ✓ The reference point that you create, which will be an ongoing focus
- ✓ The provocation to reconsider positions
- ✓ Your perspective from other companies
- ✓ The motivation that people will generate from your message
- ✓ The sense of unity, direction, and purpose that you can provide
- ✓ Your credibility
- ✓ Your personal accomplishments and results
- ✓ Your ability to serve as an exemplar
- ✓ The client's intrinsic trust in you
- ✓ Your special intellectual property
- ✓ Your fame, e.g., a commercially published, successful book

The more of these factors that apply, the more valuable you are. If you think about it, Colin Powell delivers virtually all of them. That $7,500 keynoter delivers a lot of them. How many do you deliver?

Note that my list of valuable attributes focuses mainly on the past and the future. While there are some items that are strictly in the present, such as platform skills and delivery, even these are the result of your past training, experience, and practice. In other words, there are two major aspects underlying your value to the buyer:

1. The combination of past experience and development that has produced the qualities that you convey today

2. The long-term results that the client will realize as a result of your time on the platform (or in the front of the room)

Your real worth is in the unique combination of factors that has resulted in your current value to the client and in the skills, behaviors, beliefs, and approaches that the audience will apply after your presentation that will benefit them and the business permanently. The hour itself is incidental, being nothing more than the delivery vehicle that enables your own past to benefit the audience's future.

A taxi ride from the airport is not worth $35. However, being conveyed from the airport, where you don't need to be, to the office, where you do need to be, is worth $35. A bus can take you for only $5, but it's slower, is less reliable, makes more stops, and is far less comfortable. A private limo can take you for $65, with more comfort, a private phone, better climate control, and door-to-door service. We all invest in the kind of ride that makes the most sense, and the kind that we perceive we deserve.

On a per-hour basis, a keynote is far more expensive than a full-day seminar. Someone who charges $5,000 for a keynote isn't going to charge $40,000 for a full day ($5,000 times 8 hours) if he or she offers both types of sessions. That person will probably charge around $7,500 for the full day. A keynote is much more expensive on a commodity basis because it's the limo ride—in far less time, in far more comfort, people are arriving at the destination that the buyer has chosen.

The basic process involved in speaking, from the buyer's perspective, has to be the one in Table below. It is your responsi-

Speaking Mastery

bility to educate the buyer that his or her value list is being achieved not through an hour or half day of your time, but

Speaker's Past	Current	Intervention	Client's Future
experiences	keynote	higher	productivity
education	workshop	lower	attrition
accomplishments	seminar	higher	morale
development	facilitation	improved	image
travels	training		better performance
work history			greater market share
beliefs			greater profit
victories/defeats			more growth
risks/adversity			more innovation
experimentation			problems solved
happier customers			
superior service			
process flow			

through the substantial body of work that has taken place in the past and through the results that will accrue on an ongoing basis well into the future. Few name-brand drugs that we buy cost very much to manufacture—certainly nowhere near their purchase price. However, Merck and Pfizer and Johnson & Johnson have spent billions on the research and development that finally brought the drug to the consumer in a safe, reliable, convenient form. And the drug's effect will have a long-term impact on your condition, either curing it or ameliorating it. (Eventually, both generic drugs and generic speakers pop up.)

The speaking process is no different from that of pharmaceutical research and manufacturing. We're not paying for the aspirin capsule, we're paying for the work that brought it to us and the salutary effect that it will have on our health. Buyers shouldn't be paying for the hour's speech but for the long-term processes that created its value and the longer term salutary effects on the organization.

Here is the secret to a value mindset: We use the power of our past with a transfer mechanism in the present to greatly improve the client's future. Got that? If you can understand that processflow, you'll never have trouble charging high fees.

The key to establishing high fees is to establish high future value in the eyes of the buyer. (The future could be tomorrow or next year.) Let me make this absolutely clear because most speakers focus on the wrong results. Value has very little to do with standing ovations and "smile sheets" that rate the speaker a 9.9 on a 10-point scale. The only thing that matters to the buyer is how well his or her objectives are met, and that seldom involves audience ratings unless the speaker is the one who emphasizes them. There is far more value in improved sales, lower attrition, and greater innovation in the business than there is in a speaker's rating by the audience. The rating applies to a relatively brief moment in time. The results apply to the company forever.

Most speakers, including those who "coach" and give all the advice, are charging for the first or second column in my process flow—the wrong columns! They are inputs, not value.

No company or corporate buyer has ever said, "Remember Mary Speaker? She received a 9.9 rating. What a great contribution to our business." But buyers do tend to say, "Remember the sales improvement that resulted from Mary Speaker's work? Maybe it's time to get her back in here again." Focus on your own ego, and you might get stroked. Focus on the buyer's results, and you will get repeat business.

So, it's vital to do the following to this point:

1. Understand your own value proposition.

2. Work only with true buyers.

3. Translate your value into long-term results for any given client.

4. Educate the buyer so that he or she reaches the same conclusions.

5. Only then suggest your value options.

Let's start with a simple fee system for now: a keynote, a half-day workshop, and a full-day or multiday seminar. Thus, if your keynote fee were $7,500, then your half-day fee would be $10,000, your full-day fee $15,000, and every ensuing full day $12,000. But that's just for now. We're going to quintuple that before the end of this chapter.

Ready to read on?

TAKING OUT THE MIDDLEMEN: DEALING ONLY WITH TRUE BUYERS

Note that I seldom use the word customer or client when I allude to obtaining business. That's because the buyer is the key, and speakers often don't have a clue about who the true buyer is. A buyer is someone who can authorize a check (or, in non-computer cultures, actually sign one). The buyer is usually near the top of the hierarchy in smaller organizations, but can be anywhere in larger ones. Titles are highly deceiving. (Everyone in a bank today is at least a "vice president," but nary a one of them has the authority to even waive a fee on your checking account. I call this "title inflation.")

In the speaking industry, there has been a great deal of focus on the role of the meeting planner. In most cases, a meeting planner is actually a feasibility or implementation buyer, not an economic buyer. By that I mean that the meeting planner is given a strict budget (by the real buyer) and is paid and rewarded for conserving it. Meeting planners tend to be low-level people; they are rarely involved in corporate strategy or departmental missions, and they invariably evaluate speakers as commodities to fit time frames and budgets. Meeting planners love to evaluate potential speakers by viewing demo tapes for a few minutes, making visceral decisions based on such ephemera as a funny story, stage movement, and appearance.

Speakers' bureaus tend to deal through meeting planners, middlemen (consistency with "middlemen"?) dealing with middlemen, sort of like "Middle Earth," and kind of like hobbits. If you work with bureaus, you won't miss these potential buyers because the bureau will find them for you.

But for your own approaches, eschew the meeting planners and focus on the economic buyers, who themselves are focused on results. They are the ones to whom you can make your value/results appeal. Since they are paid to achieve results themselves, they will find the money to pay for anyone who can help them engender those results. The equation for them is simple: ROI (return on investment).

Whenever possible, market and sell to economic buyers. If you find that you've been introduced to a feasibility or implementation buyer, use that entry point to gain access to the economic buyer. Bureaus will otherwise attend to the meeting planner market, although the good ones will pursue economic buyers as well. Your strategy should look something like that depicted in below.

The primary thrust of the speaker (and of any marketing or staff personnel who are employed in these pursuits) should be to establish a relationship with the economic buyer. A secondary thrust should be toward those bureaus that can place

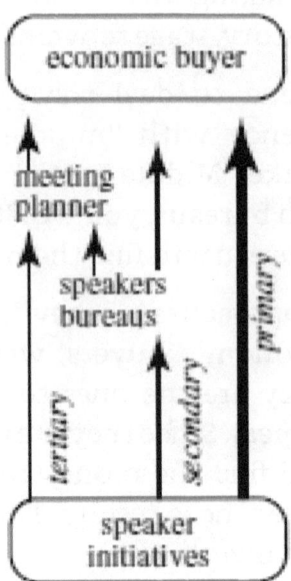

Speaker Marketing Priorities

you with economic buyers, although they will invariably also work with meeting planners. Only a tertiary thrust—meaning if there is time or as a result of serendipity—should be geared toward the meeting planner on the chance that this path may lead to the economic buyer. In my experience, most speakers reverse this sequence, thereby securing a poor return on their scarce resources. So, our steps might really look like this:

1. Understand your own value package.

2. Translate your value into long-term results for any given client.

3. Find the economic buyer in your target customer.

4. Educate the buyer so that he or she reaches the same conclusions.

5. Only then suggest your value options.

How do you know a true buyer when you see one? Is it like the yeti, something that is rarely seen, but leaves just enough tracks in the snow to suggest a sentient being? Or is it Waldo, hidden in some crowd awaiting your scrutiny?

My economic buyers have had titles such as director, manager, business process consultant, vice president, owner, and, of course, CEO. At higher levels, it's fairly easy to tell. You might be talking to the vice president of sales who is interested in a speaker for his or her sales conference. There's not much detective work required. But what if you're talking to a sales director who tells you that she has been given the task of securing the speakers for the meeting? How do you tell if this is the economic buyer or merely a feasibility buyer, without offending her?

Here are the questions I've found useful in ferreting out the real economic buyer. You don't need to ask all of them, and you should choose those that best fit your style, since I'm prone to simply ask, "Are you the one who's investing the money?"

Questions to Find the Economic Buyer

- ✓ Whose budget is supporting this investment?
- ✓ Who will evaluate the final results?
- ✓ To whom do the participants all commonly report?
- ✓ Whose objectives are at stake?
- ✓ Which executive will open and/or close (be featured at) the meeting?
- ✓ Who approves the final agenda?
- ✓ Will you make a decision or a recommendation to someone else?
- ✓ If there are conflicts over the agenda, who makes the final call?
- ✓ Who is most affected by the success or failure of the participants?

Committees are seldom economic buyers. By definition, they

are evaluators and recommenders. You can ask these questions in as blatant (New York) or subtle (California) a fashion as you wish, as long as you do ask them. Too often, we're so delighted merely to have been considered for a speaking engagement that we fall all over ourselves trying to impress whoever will see us. That's fine if we want to secure jobs, but it doesn't contribute anything if we want to create a million dollar business.

(Incidentally, sometimes we find ourselves magically with the economic buyer at the outset. Here's some complex advice: don't leave. It's not uncommon for the speaker to react to the initial contact by accepting delegation to a feasibility buyer. If you actively participate in the intent to delegate yourself downward, you'll experience a vertiginous drop through the organization, landing dazed and bruised in the office of someone who will ask you, as soon as you've revived, "So, how much can you reduce your fee if we cut the slot from 2 hours to 45 minutes?")

And what happens when we meticulously apply the questions and discover that we are, indeed, dealing only with a gatekeeper who resists allowing us to talk to the economic buyer? We've all encountered the palace guards who bloviate about how busy the management is, but whose sworn duty is to protect the decision makers from actually receiving information that might lead to a high-quality decision. Do we resign ourselves to the ignominy, or do we scale the ramparts?

Get out your ladders and climbing gear. Here's how you convince the gatekeeper to either open the gates or get out of the way while you open them. Leverage Points to Get to the Economic Buyer

- ✓ I have to ensure that his or her objectives are met.
- ✓ I have to be sure that there are no unreasonable expectations.
- ✓ I have to ensure that the full value of what I can deliver is understood.

- ✓ I must tailor my approach to his or her style/theme/philosophy/agenda.
- ✓ Ethically, I must see the person who is investing the money.
- ✓ It's unfair for you to do my marketing for me.
- ✓ There are technical details that only I can explain.
- ✓ It's imperative that I hear his or her strategy and tactics.
- ✓ You and I can collaborate once we've both received his or her advice.
- ✓ I do this with every client. It's why I've been recommended to him or her.
- ✓ This is what outstanding professionals do in this business.
- ✓ It's for his or her protection. Objectives sometimes change.
- ✓ It's a strict quality policy, and I can't work with him or her unless we meet.

In the event that all of these fail, you may want to simply contact the economic buyer and advise that person of the same types of issues. You do risk irritating the gatekeeper and perhaps losing the potential business. However, no risk, no reward. It's simply that important to find the economic buyer and secure your agreement with him or her because only that person can appreciate your value package and the long-term results for the organization in terms of an appropriate investment.

PROVIDING THE CHOICE OF "YESES"

I've spent the entire first half of this chapter leading up to fee structure, and we're not quite there yet. That's because your fee strategy is irrelevant if you're dealing with the wrong people or if you're not in a position to establish value and results.

On the assumption that you've accomplished that, however, we're at the final step:

1. Understand your own value package.

2. Translate your value into long-term results for any given client.

3. Find the economic buyer in your target customer.

4. Educate the buyer so that he or she reaches the same conclusions.

5. Only then suggest your value options.

You never want the buyer to be making the decision as to whether or not to use your services. You want the buyer to be making the decision as to how to use your services. To accomplish that, you must provide the buyer with options. You control this dynamic. If you provide options, the buyer will consider them. If you don't, it's unlikely that the buyer will say, "Why don't we develop some options that provide me with a range of ways in which to use you?"

This is not abstruse reasoning. The buyer will do what's in his or her best interest. You must manage the relationship so that what's in your self-interest is in the buyer's self-interest: hiring you.

An Example

Let's suppose that the buyer is considering you for a two-hour concurrent session at an annual conference. The buyer has budgeted for six speakers at $3,500 each in the three concurrent sessions and $6,500 each for keynoters to open and close. Here are some options you might propose:

- ✓ Conduct one concurrent session as planned for $3,500.
- ✓ Conduct two of the concurrent sessions on different topics for $6,000, saving the client $1,000.
- ✓ Present one of the keynotes and a concurrent session for $8,000, saving the client $2,000.
- ✓ Present the concurrent session and facilitate breakout groups when the participants are later divided into working teams for $5,000.
- ✓ Present the concurrent session and moderate a customer panel that the client had planned for later in the program for $5,000.
- ✓ Use any permutations of the foregoing options.

However, there is a far more powerful way to build speaking fees into project riches.

TURNING AN EVENT INTO A PROCESS AND TRIPLING YOUR SUCCESS

A standard exercise that I insist on in my coaching of speakers is to create a list of everything that they can do prior to, during, and after a session. Many speakers include these elements anyway, since their low self-esteem drives them to throw in everything but washing the dog to justify their fee. None of this will be terribly new, until you see what I'm about to do with it.

Here is a synopsis of what most people tell me. Your lists may differ based upon your topic, background, and focus.

Prior to Event	During Event	After Event
Interview attendees brief with buyer	Deliver presentation	De-
Interview customers Follow-up sessions	Provide visuals	aids
Interview suppliers page access	Provide handouts	Web
Shop the business by e-mail	Book signing	Coaching

Shop the competition   Partners' program
Coaching by phone

Survey   Breakout groups   Survey

Customize materials   Electronic summaries

Interview board4   Newsletter

Submit plans/review   Send best practices

Talk to other speakers   Follow-up
materials

Critique the agenda

You can see where this is going. Instead of an "event," you now have a process for improvement. Instead of throwing, the kitchen sink into the pot, you're offering the buyer a menu of options.

"What will the fee be?" you're asked.

"I can't tell yet, but why don't you select the value that appeals to you during our overall time together, and I'll create a fee based on your needs and preferences."

I guarantee you—guarantee you—that if you take this structure and organize every speaking opportunity, whether keynote or training, around it, you will quintuple your fees over the course of a year. That means that you must overcome the mentality that "I'm not worth it" and adopt the mentality that "I have tremendous value to offer, and I'd be remiss if I didn't provide everything I can for the buyer's consideration."

Note that this doesn't work unless you're talking to a buyer. A human resource person will simply ask you to do it all for the lowest fee possible.

Buyers may love to reduce fees, but they hate to reduce value. Once you introduce significant value, buyers want it. This is an emotional decision. Logic makes people think; emotion makes them act. On the trust "pyramid," you'll find this progression:

Emotional

Intellectual

Affiliative

Expert

Referral

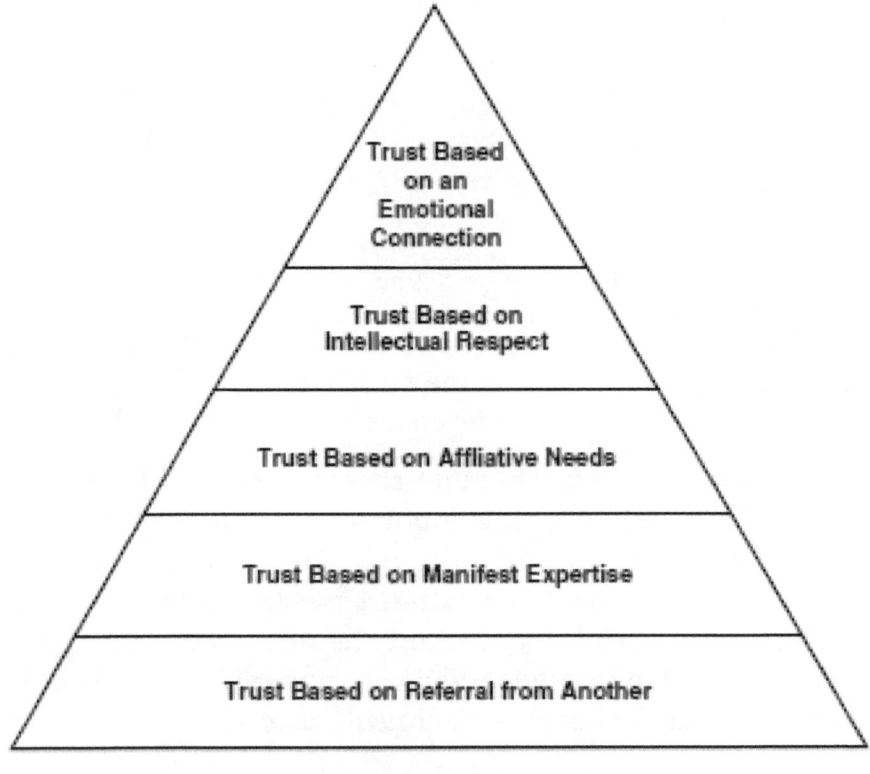

The Trust Pyramid

Being referred by a trusted source is important; being seen as an expert is comforting; filling a desire to have an affiliation is significant; holding high intellectual status is imposing, but creating an emotional bond is invaluable.

No buyer says, "Listen up, I was able to get the cheapest speaker in the country. I might have obtained his services for less, but I felt sorry for him. I want you to hang on his every word."

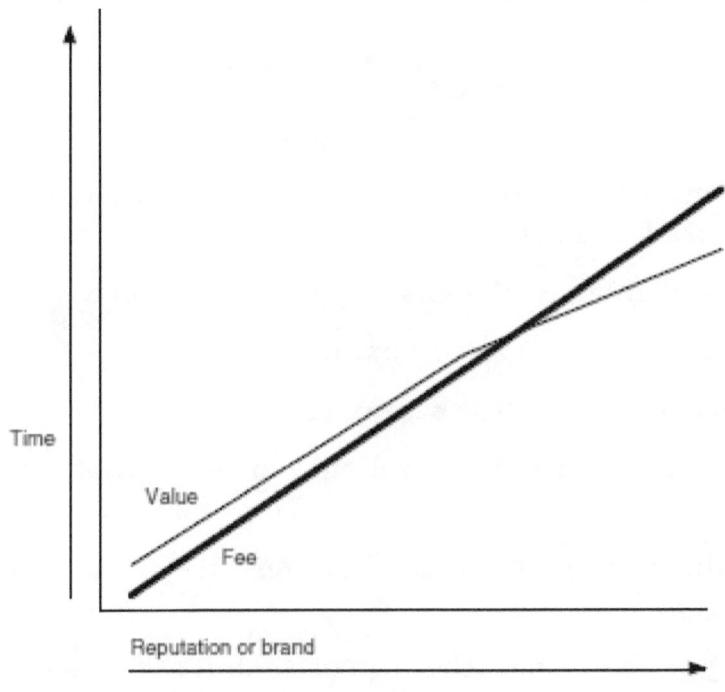

When Value Follows Fee

Instead, they say what Curt Nelson, CEO of Silicon Space, said when he asked his people how much they thought I was costing to address them for a few hours at a meeting. Their guesses ranged from $1,500 to $3,500, with one executive wonderin, if that included lunch.\

"He has charged me $18,500," said Curt, "so listen up!!" Buyers have egos, too.

40 WAYS TO INCREASE YOUR FEES

Here are 40 ways to increase your fees, in addition to the model I've already provided:

1. Establish value collaboratively with the client.

2. Base your fees on value, not on the task.

3. Never use time as the basis of your value.

4. Don't stop with what the client wants—find out what the client needs.

5. Think of the fourth sale first—fees are cumulative, not situational.

6. Engage the client in the diagnosis—don't be prescriptive.

7. Never voluntarily offer options to reduce fees.

8. Add a premium if you personally "do it all."

9. If you're forced to consider fee reduction, reduce value first.

10. Provide options every time: the choice of "yeses."

11. Always provide an option that is comprehensive and over budget.

12. As early as possible, ask the QGTRIHF (Question Guaranteed to Result in Higher Fees): "What are your objectives?"

13. Broaden objectives as appropriate to increase value.

Speaking Mastery

14. Ensure that the client is aware of the full range of your services.

15. If something is not on your playing field, subcontract it.

16. Always ask yourself, "Why me, why now, why in this manner?"

17. Determine how many options the buyer perceives other than you.

18. Use proposals as confirmations, not explorations.

19. When asked prematurely about fees, reply, "I don't know."

20. If you must lower fees, seek a quid pro quo from the buyer.

21. Do not accept troublesome, unpleasant, or suspicious business.

22. When collaborating or subcontracting, use objective apportionment.

23. Any highly paid employee must bring in new business, not merely deliver.

24. Seek out new economic buyers laterally during your projects.

25. It is better to do something pro bono than to do it for a low fee.

26. Fees have nothing to do with supply and demand, only with value.

27. If you are unaware of the current market fee ranges, you're undercharging.

28. Psychologically, higher fees create higher value in the buyer's mind.

29. Value can include subjective as well as objective measures.

30. Introduce new value to existing clients to raise fees in these

accounts.

31. Do not accept referral business on the same basis as the referent.

32. When forced into phases, offer partial rebates to guarantee future business.

33. At least every two years, consider jettisoning the bottom 15 percent of your business.

34. Start with payment terms that are maximally beneficial to you every time.

35. Offer incentives for one-time, full payments.

36. Never accept payment subject to conditions to be met upon completion.

37. Focus on improvement, not problem solving.

38. Provide proactive ideas, benchmarking, and best practices from experience.

39. Practice stating and explaining your fees.

40. Always be prepared to walk away from business.

You'd have a hard time convincing me that at least half of these points don't apply to your situation and business.

INCREASING FEE VELOCITY

There's one more aspect to improving fees that most speakers neglect: the velocity of the fee. This means that you want to get your fee into your bank as rapidly as possible, but the default position of speakers is often "pay me whenever you feel like it." The terms and conditions of your engagement should be stipulated after conceptual agreement on outcomes and value so that they are merely an afterthought for the buyer. But if you don't establish payment terms, some purchasing agent in the bowels of the client organization is ready—and paid—to do so.

Always try to get paid in full in advance. You won't always be able to, but you will never be paid this way if you don't ask. Simply state that your policy is full fee in advance to secure the date and begin any preparatory activities, such as presentation design, materials customization, participant interviews, and so forth.

If you can't get your full fee in advance, you may want to try a soft incentive, such as a 5 or 10 percent discount if the fee is paid in advance. (Don't offer this if the presentation date is imminent.) Such a discount is important for two reasons:

1. You will be holding the money and using it for a long period, sometimes as much as a year in advance.

2. The client cannot cancel your engagement if you are holding the money.

Note: Many bureaus have a "policy" of holding your fees "in escrow" until after you deliver the presentation and the client is happy. Simply don't do business with someone with this kind of benighted mentality. The client is YOURS, not the bureau's, which is merely the middleman. Your payment terms are up to you.

Demand, as a minimum, a 50 percent deposit, with the balance to be paid prior to the time of the presentation. That's right, you get an envelope before you show up. Some bureaus will demand a 50 percent deposit and keep all of it until your presentation as a "guarantee." Tell them to take a walk. If a bureau collects a 50 percent deposit, it should keep its 25 percent full commission and forward the balance to you immediately.

If a bureau places you and collects the deposit, the balance should be payable to you at the presentation, not to the bureau (which will further delay payment, sometimes for months —some bureaus even demand that expense reimbursement go through them).

I don't advise ever accepting less than a 50 percent deposit, or a bureau collecting its 25 percent commission, with the remainder being received on the presentation date. Anything less is not a collaboration and leaves you vulnerable to cancellation, delay, late payments, disputed costs, client internal turmoil, and so forth.

Guarantee your work in writing, but make your contract noncancelable in writing as the quid pro quo. This is a business. Businesses turn a profit. (I had four such full deposits prior to 9/11. I offered every client its money back in the wake of the tragedy. Every one told me that it would reschedule; some took over a year to do so, but each one did, and I kept the money and the clients.)

To summarize: base your fees on the value you bring to the client's objectives; provide for options (value packages) in the context of a process flow, so that the client can decide how best to use you and not whether to use you, and increase the velocity of the ensuing payment in every way possible through aggressive terms. If you do that, you'll have the processes in place to make a million dollars. Let's turn now to how you attract that kind of business.

SUMMARY

Fees should be based on value. Even a "bare bones" keynote request has the potential for advance work, concurrent work, and follow-up work. Don't view what you do as an "event," but rather as a "process."

At a minimum, set your fees aggressively for a short, medium, and longer presentation. These fees should not be based on your tenure in the profession, but rather on your brand, your intellectual property, and the value you deliver. The easiest, best, and most lucrative way to do this is to deal directly with economic buyers, not with middlemen.

Speakers' bureaus and meeting planners are not organized to maximize your fees or even to maximize your success. The former work on a volume basis, trying to place as many people as they can in the mistaken belief that the client belongs to them and that speakers are merely hired hands instead of talent. The latter are paid and given incentives to minimize costs, irrespective of quality or results.

You can get so good, so much in demand, and so talked about that value will follow fees—buyers will expect to get what they pay for, just as they do with a Bentley car or a Baume & Mercier watch.

If you want to make a million in the speaking profession, focus on these two keys: work only with true buyers, not middlemen; and focus on the process and its outcomes, not the time or event. If you do, you'll be ahead of about 85 percent of the speakers out there.

MODERN MARKETING

I DON'T CARE ABOUT THE COST

IT'S IMPORTANT that you attract business because

- ✓ Very few people buy from "cold calls" in this business.
- ✓ You don't have to prove yourself or present credentials.
- ✓ There is minimal cost of acquisition.
- ✓ Fees simply don't matter.

I could go on, but that's more than enough. You want to attract the right clients—those that are amenable and appropriate for the fee structures discussed in Chapter 4. Fortunately, I can help you do that right here.

THE MAGIC AND MYTH OF THE INTERNET

Let me annoy as many of you as I can immediately: your Web site is not a sales tool.

Oh, my, what about all those Internet marketing gurus? Well, they're wrong about Web sites (and a lot of other stuff, but we don't have time for that here).

Your Web site is a credibility statement. That is, buyers— true buyers—might go there to get some additional information once they hear of you, read something about you, meet with you, and so forth. Only nonbuyers "troll" the Internet looking for speakers, and they will send a generic communication, such as: "We are looking for presenters at the National Hot Air and Persiflage Association annual convention. If you're interested, please go to www.gasbag.edu and fill out the presenter's form."

What this means is that your site needs to do only two things —two things!—well and quickly: tell the buyer what's in it for him or her, and justify it with testimonials from his or her peers.

Formula for Web Site Success

1. State your value proposition prominently (e.g., "I reduce the cost of new client acquisition while decreasing closing times").

2. State quickly what's in it for the buyer, e.g., your people will:

- ✓ Master the four steps of the "immediate close."
- ✓ Rebut resistance in the four main objections dimensions.
- ✓ Create larger sales per new customer.
- ✓ Learn to close sales on the telephone.
- ✓ Generate more profit per client.

3. Have at least two prominent testimonials, preferably video testimonials and/or rotating print testimonials.

4. On succeeding pages, include your position papers, credentials, clients, case studies, speaking topics, whatever. But these are all subordinate to the value to be found immediately on the home page. Think of your home page as the opening two minutes of a speech, during which people decide whether to pay close attention thereafter.

5. It's as simple as that.

Social media platforms, at least as of this writing, are for fun and for looking up old school chums, but not for marketing professional services. (Would you hire a speaker who solicited you on social media? Most high-level buying decisions are made on the basis of peer-to-peer referrals.)

Search engine optimization (SEO) and placing ads on Google and similar sources (or paying for positioning) are wastes of time and money, because buyers aren't seeking you on the Internet. Besides, the more you publish, are interviewed, and speak (see the discussion of Market Gravity later in this chapter), the more you'll be automatically elevated on the search engines. Stop worrying about this, and never pay for it.

However, there are some simple actions that can pay dividends. For example, always have a full signature file (including your address—if a stalker wants to kill you, there are otherways to find you), and include a brief promotional statement (e.g., "Cited as the best speaker on global leadership in the manufacturing arena—Chicago Tribune") and a reference to your Web site, blog, newsletter, or other source.

If your expertise is in team building, for example, create an electronic newsletter that is provocative and will brand you: Jim Pay's PAYDAY, the newsletter for high-performing team leadership.

People complain to me, "There are so many newsletters; won't mine get lost in the crowd?" Yes, if you're dull. There are so many newsletters because people read them. (Burger King builds burger joints across the street from McDonald's because it knows that people in the area are buying burgers!) Competition opens markets, it doesn't confine markets.

Pull together a list, no matter how modest at first, and create an online, consistent newsletter. If your list grows, consider a listserv, which will allow automatic subscriptions, cancellations, changes, and so forth, as well as distribution with one simple paste.

While the social media platforms are mostly for informal chats (and can be huge time dumps), blogs are something else. There are 200 million blogs in the world as I write this, and 99 percent of them are awful—self-indulgent, derivative, outright plagiarized, ungrammatical, blatant self-promotion, and so on. Many of them don't even reveal their source, and quite a few are just excuses to sell advertisements.

However, if you are provocative; use text, audio, and video; and post regularly (e.g., at least three times per week— many blogs go months without updating), you can use this as a springboard to refer people to your business and results. Buyers do, on occasion, subscribe to blogs that focus on their areas of interest (e.g., The Strategist Next Door).

Use the Internet as one aspect of your promotion, but don't assume that it's all things to all people. Most of the greatest advocates for Internet marketing make their money by selling Internet marketing services, if you get my drift.

WORKING (OR NOT) WITH BUREAUS AND AVOID BEING A HIRED HAND

The key to riches in the speaking business is working smart, not working hard. That means that you need to examine your own basic beliefs, understandings, assumptions, and implicit approaches to the business, since there's a distinct possibility that some of them are inaccurate and a couple may be plain wrong. That's because there are more people giving advice (and charging for it) in the speaking business than there are good speakers.

The last time anyone looked, coaching was a leveraging position, meaning that there are a multitude of excellent players created by a superb coach. When there is mediocre coaching, there is usually a myriad of very average players. But in no circumstances is there a rational reason to have legions of good coaches and a resultant swarm of undistinguished players. There are relatively few excellent speakers in the land (otherwise, fee competition would keep prices low, and my advice in the previous chapter about charging for value would be commonplace), which leads me to believe that the hordes of coaches aren't that hot, either.

One of the worst of the assumptions that even veteran speakers labor under is that a relationship with a speakers' bureau is mandatory and that the parameters of such a relationship are dictated by the bureau, which can be very choosy about whom it represents. Here are some facts about the bureau relationship that apply to all of us, whether we've never been asked, never chose to work with them, work with them occasionally, or get virtually all of our engagements through them (which is exceedingly rare).

Musts for a Successful Bureau Relationship: Speaker Requirements

1. Establish a relationship with the owner. Others may place you and market you, but you can tell if the bureau's values are compatible with yours only by working with the principal.

2. Request and receive references and examples of the bureau's marketing materials. Don't accept claims at face value. Ask if this quality represents you well.

3. Retain your identity on the materials and literature that you provide for marketing. If the bureau doesn't trust you, then don't get involved with it.

4. Avoid mandatory co-marketing investments. Options to take out listings, showcase, exhibit, and so on are fine and valuable, as long as you can pick and choose. But too many bureaus are trying to earn money from speakers and not for speakers.

5. Clarify that you will speak to prospects directly and early when this is needed to determine how to help close the business (and if it's right for your skills).

6. Expect a callback on the same business day (or the next morning) when you leave a message with the bureau. You're entitled to professional responsiveness.

7. Require that "holds" (tentative bookings) be managed carefully and removed from your calendar as soon as the bureau determines that the business will not close.

8. Ensure that all fees in excess of the bureau's commission are paid directly to you at the time of receipt and that the client directly reimburses you for your expenses.

9. Request flexibility in commissions for spin-off business, multiple bookings, ancillary consulting work, and related situations that merit reduced commissions.

10. Avoid exclusive arrangements. Only by allowing numerous bureaus to represent you will you ensure your own flexibility and find your own best deals.

Musts for a Successful Bureau Relationship: Bureau Requirements

The excellent bureaus have legitimate needs that speakers must adhere to, especially if a trusting relationship is to be built. A great deal of this relies on on ethical and professional behavior, which, unfortunately, isn't always in great supply.

1. Be honest about your capabilities. Don't accept assignments unless you can serve the client well. Exceed expectations. The bureau's reputation is its main asset.

2. Be original. Don't use others' materials, and don't use shopworn generic stories. Clients who hire speakers can usually spot these instantly.

3. Arrive early and stay late. Let the local coordinator know that you've arrived, and don't rush off during the applause. Avoid tight connections and last-minute arrivals.

4. Be honest about outcomes. If there were problems, whether technical, interpersonal, or logistical, tell the bureau immediately.

Speaking Mastery

5. Keep your materials up to date and professional. Provide contemporary testimonials, quality brochures, and effective handouts.

6. Join in win/win co-marketing. It can make sense for you to appear in a special mailing or create a voice-mail sample of your speaking. You're in this together.

7. Speak to prospects quickly whenever requested. Good bureaus know when a few words from the speaker can close the deal. Don't keep the buyer waiting.

8. Recommend other fine speakers to the bureau. This is not a zero-sum game. The more the bureau succeeds, the more it can invest in your success.

9. Scrupulously forward spin-off business (business leads or closed deals gained during a bureau placement). This is a contractual and an ethical requirement.

10. Maintain consistency in your fee structure (although it may be highly diverse), and provide lengthy advance notice if scheduled fees are to be raised. Having said all that, bureaus should be a minor part of your marketing cosmos.

TRADE ASSOCIATIONS: MAKE MONEY AND MARKET CONCURRENTLY

When you speak at a trade association, you are being explicitly or implicitly endorsed by an objective third party—the trade association. In most cases, you're also being paid to be there, which means that you're making money while you market and you're seen as highly valuable.

My idea of the hierarchy of highly leveraged marketing through sponsors and third parties follows. The characteristics of the most potentially rewarding third-party sponsors are:

- ✓ Full and normal fees are paid to the speaker.
- ✓ The audience includes significant buyers for your services.
- ✓ The audience is large.
- ✓ The event is prestigious and the sponsor is highly regarded.
- ✓ There are other "draws" on the agenda.
- ✓ You have a general session, not a concurrent session.
- ✓ You can sell products and services at the event.

As you can see, a local nonprofit group is probably looking for some sage advice and professional platform skills, but the audience usually will contain, at best, recommenders. But at a national trade association meeting, all of my conditions can be met.

The Hierarchy of Third-Party Sponsorship National trade associations

- ✓ Health Industries Distributors Association
- ✓ International Association for Financial Planners
- ✓ American Bankers Association

Local and regional trade associations (or chapters)

- ✓ Minneapolis Personnel Association
- ✓ Houston Chapter, American Institute of Architects
- ✓ Tennessee Recreational Vehicle Association

Management extension programs

- ✓ Universities, colleges, junior colleges
- ✓ Private programs (The Learning Connection)
- ✓ Government support (Small Business Administration)

Local nonprofit business groups

- ✓ Rotary
- ✓ Chamber of Commerce
- ✓ Better Business Bureau

Local nonprofit community groups

- ✓ Service clubs
- ✓ Youth groups
- ✓ Parent-teacher leagues

Trade associations have a lot of money. They will often have a meeting planner who is much more powerful than his or her private-sector counterpart because the trade association's raison d'^etre is the education of its members, so conferences and conventions are the place to demonstrate to the members that their dues and obligations are quite worthwhile. You will be dealing with either the executive director of the association or a meeting planner who is also an officer of the organization.

Don't let anyone kid you; trade associations pay as much as, if not more than, private-sector meetings. Here are 12 tips for successfully marketing to trade associations and successfully delivering a speech to the membership that will result in leveraged business from the attendees.

TIPS TO LEVERAGE THE TRADE ASSOCIATION MARKETPLACE

1. Talk to members first. Learn about their concerns and issues. If you are targeting the National Association of Music Merchants, visit some local members' retail stores and talk to the owners.

2. Demonstrate a unique nonindustry perspective. These conferences are blanketed with speakers with content knowledge, and they're usually deadly dull. Establish conversancy in the field, but introduce your fresh, nonindustry perspective. Your value is in world-class best practices. (I was a huge hit speaking about strategy at the American Feed and Grain Lot convention because everyone else was speaking about the innards of animals.)

3. Create an intelligence file. Using your regular business reading, the Internet, and reference resources, generate a "dossier" on the industry's strengths and weaknesses, its past, present, and likely future.

4. Orient your approach toward the future. Trade association members are thirsty for help in making sense out of changing times, particularly in volatile industries (e.g., health care,

telecommunications, and travel). Don't tell them what they already know.

5. Be provocative. Don't be afraid to be contrarian. Give people something to talk about. You want your name mentioned in the halls. (One association executive rushed up to me to tell me, "You were a hit in the ladies room!" You never know about all the private measurement devices that buyers use in this business.)

6. Create visual aids and handouts that mention the industry. You don't have to create an entirely new speech, but you should insert examples, stories, anecdotes, visuals, and aspects of your handouts (if you use them) that embrace the industry. This helps the learning and greatly increases the likelihood of spin-off business.

7. Let the audience know that you've done your homework. I almost always include some segments in which I say, "I polled some of the members at this convention and asked them what advice they'd give someone who was new to your business. Over 80 percent said, 'Save your money!'"

8. Create a meeting-specific handout. This could be a single sheet, a copy of your slides, or detailed support for your presentation. Make it something that participants will want to keep. Put the conference date and the title of your speech on the cover. In addition, put your name and every piece of contact information on every page (in case individual pages are photocopied and circulated back home).

9. Offer to deliver multiple sessions. Even highly paid veteran speakers will gladly do this. The association likes to provide the keynoter, for example, in the more intimate setting of a concurrent session. The association can save money—and you can earn more—by using you three times instead of using three people one time each.

10. Parlay your trade association appearances. Include

trade association publicity, testimonials, appearance dates, interviews, and so forth prominently in your media kit. Trade association speaking, as you've seen, is a somewhat specialized skill. If you've mastered it, the accolades can provide ready access to more and more associations.

11. Record it. Many large meetings feature projections on screens, and such equipment can automatically record for you. If that's not the case, ask about the facility or organization recording your presentation. Worst case, consider paying for it yourself. (Get professional advice, for example, using two cameras, avoiding time-sensitive references, wardrobe, and so forth.) You can use this for marketing, product sales, selfimprovement, and other purposes.

12. Meet the board. Either interview the board members or meet them on site if they're present, because almost every board member of a professional association is a business owner or executive and a prospective buyer of your services. Offer to build in their comments and/or debrief them, but whatever you do, try to make sure that you develop a relationship that you can nurture post-speech.

Trade associations are ideal venues for new and veteran speakers. Go after the executive director with a press kit, a demo video (if you have one), an introduction from a third party (if you can get one), and a follow-up phone call, all emphasizing what you can do to improve the membership's condition. Offer to do interviews for the association's publications and/or contribute articles. These are rich mines of speaking wealth.

WHERE AND HOW TO PUBLISH

If you want to make it big in the speaking profession, you have to publish. Articles in major media will do the following:

- ✓ Enhance your visibility and credibility
- ✓ Provide solid content for your media kit
- ✓ Force you to continually generate new ideas and validate old ones
- ✓ Gain entry into more and more publications through repute
- ✓ Provide access to other media (radio, TV, Internet)
- ✓ Generate leads
- ✓ Provide handouts for your sessions
- ✓ Form the basis for future books
- ✓ Form the basis for future products
- ✓ Transform intellectual capital into intellectual property

If you've never published, use the "staircase" technique shown in Figure below. It begins with a local column for the weekly community newspaper and leads to the local daily (Podunk Pendulum), the regional daily (Hartford Courant), the state magazine (Rhode Island Monthly), the national publication (Bottom Line), and the "media of record" (New York Times,

Speaking Mastery

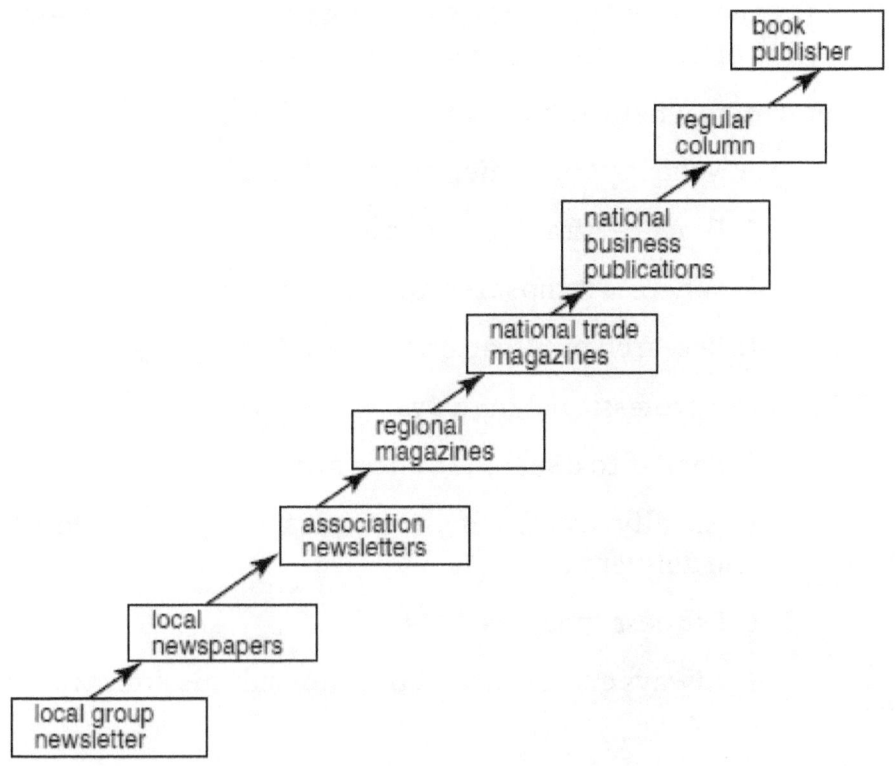

The staircase method for publishing.

Wall Street Journal). In other words, parlay what you do, using tear sheets and columns from the first publications to progressively sell editors of larger publications.7

How to Get an Article Published

I. Determine what subject you want to write about.

    A. Why are you the person to comment on the topic?

    B. How will this subject enhance your business, repute, or standing?

    C. Why is the subject relevant at this time (and for the next several months)?

Don't be afraid to be contrarian. The world doesn't

need another piece on "left-brain vs. right-brain thinking" or "the seven delta approach to quality."

II. Determine where you want to publish the article.

    A. Who is your audience, and what does it read?

    B. Don't be afraid to ask your audience!

    C. Where is it most reasonable for you to be successful?

    D. Research publications and study their style.

III. Prepare a professional inquiry.

    A. Send it to a specific editor's attention.

    B. Specify what, why, examples, uniqueness, length, and delivery date.

    C. Request specifications.

    D. Always enclose a SASE8 if your submission is in hard copy.

    E. Cite credentials—yours and the article's.

This step must be more carefully executed than the actual article!

IV. Write it like a pro.

    A. Use specific examples, names, and places.

    B. Write it yourself, but solicit critiques.

    C. Write it to the specifications.

    D. Make sure that you include autobiographical data at the end.

    E. Request free reprints, reprint permission, or discounted reprints.

    F. Don't self-promote; let the substance do it for you.

G. If rejected: resubmit, resubmit, resubmit, resubmit, resubmit.

Use prior articles as credentials to write newer ones.

SOME OTHER COMMENTS

Don't overwrite. Write what's on your mind without worrying about the great American novel. When you edit, you'll find that the piece is amazingly good. Attribute things that you borrow, but don't try to dazzle your reader with superfluous references. Be critical and analytical. Readers responds best to provocation and the opportunity to look at things in a new way. When in doubt, start a new paragraph. Use graphics when appropriate, and try to load in the metaphors and similes.

Tell people what they need to know, not everything that you know!

The great debate is about whether or not to self-publish books. I've self-published as well as published commercially. My criteria are simple: self-publish books when

- ✓ You want a product to sell with maximum profit.
- ✓ You want a handout for your training sessions.
- ✓ You have a clearly defined niche market.
- ✓ You have a very powerful brand that will draw readers.
- ✓ You want to capitalize on a time-sensitive event or window.

But publish only through a known commercial publisher when

- ✓ You want maximum credibility with buyers (especially corporate).

- ✓ You want to improve your credibility as an authority.
- ✓ You want maximum distribution channels.
- ✓ You want to maximize your chances for foreign translation.

Sometimes a commercially published book will earn considerable royalties, and sometimes a self-published book will gain you credibility. But not usually. Notice that ego stroking is not on either list. There are a lot of bad books published commercially, and most self-published books are awful. If you need your ego stroked, buy a dog. If you need to tell people that you're an author, yet you have nothing to say that will sell a publisher, use the money you would have invested in the vanity publishing to secure the services of a therapist. You're not a driver unless you can drive a car, and you're not an author unless someone else pays to publish your stuff.

And NEVER invest in a scheme where you have one chapter in a book with famous "names" authoring the others. That is laughably transparent and makes money only for those who organize the "opportunity."

Harsh? Yes. Reality? Also yes.

Here's my route for getting a book published commercially once you've ascended the staircase. Book publishing is slightly easier when you have a long track record of articles and columns to support it, but these are not prerequisites. The most important thing is convincing the publisher (or your agent) that your book will sell, and the way to achieve that is to do your own homework, because the editor hasn't the time or the inclination to do it for you. It is difficult to get your first book published, but with a targeted, systematic approach, it's much easier than most people think. Follow these guidelines.

HOW TO GET A BOOK PUBLISHED

I. Determine what it is you have to say.

    A. Your particular expertise from your education, experience, training, or circumstances.

    B. Your ability to "pull together" disparate things that others haven't.

    C. Your ideas, concepts, theories, and innovations.

    D. Your work with clients.

If you have nothing constructive to contribute, don't write a word.

II. Determine which publishers are most likely to agree with you.

    A. Examine their current books in print.

    B. Request their specifications.

    C. Ask people in the business.

Do not vanity publish or self-publish—it's a waste of time and no one's impressed—unless you apply the previous criteria and they pertain to you.

III. Prepare a treatment for the publisher's (or agent's) review.

    A. Why you?

Speaking Mastery

> B. Why this topic?
>
> C. Why this topic handled in this manner?
>
> D. What competitive works are extant, and why is yours needed?
>
> E. Who is the audience?
>
> F. When would the manuscript be ready?
>
> G. What are its special features (e.g., endorsements, self-tests, etc.)?
>
> H. Provide at least the introduction and one chapter, a table of contents, and summaries of the other chapters.

If you can't sell it to the publisher, you'll never sell it to the reader.

IV. Write it like a pro.

> A. Invite clients and/or respected authorities to contribute.
>
> B. Use sophisticated fonts and formatting.
>
> C. Don't use a "ghost." If someone else writes your book, why does anyone need you?
>
> D. Always take the reader's viewpoint.
>
> E. Schedule your writing sessions just as you would your other responsibilities.
>
> F. Use trusted others to review, critique, and suggest.
>
> G. Always attribute anything that's not yours.
>
> H. Keep it "future-current"—remember, it will be published a year after your submission.

What is published represents your values. Are you proud of what you've written?

Dr. Dennis Mulumba

Some Other Comments

Don't become discouraged—keep submitting, and find out why you've been rejected. And remember, a successful business book sells about 7,500 copies! Don't expect to be on Oprah the next Monday. Finally, read contracts carefully because they will specify the author's discount, planned promotion, expenses you may incur, and so on. For example, you can often negotiate the indexing costs to be transferred from you to the publisher. Run the whole thing by your attorney.

Publishing will, at first, require a substantial investment of time. However, you can usually find that time on airplanes and in distant hotel rooms. Once you've broken into the field, you'll find it easier and easier to publish, both because your skills are developing and because your credibility is growing.

The staircase method is useful to ensure that you also grow as an author and avoid the success trap of publishing repeatedly for a limited audience.

THE MARKET GRAVITY CYCLE

Here is a synopsis of Market Gravity. A new speaker should have a minimum of four routes underway. A veteran should have at least a dozen. In no particular order:

- ✓ Referrals. Referrals are the platinum standard in this business. While it's nice to have your name in the hat when someone requests "a superb speaker on sales excellence," it's far better when they say, "I hear from a good friend over at Acme—get me Joan Martin!"
- ✓ Commercially published books. The gold standard is a book from a major publisher. Many people who have hired me have never read the book that attracted them to me. But they saw "Real Estate Investing to make millions," "Entrepreneur Success Handbook," and my name Dr. Dennis Mulumba. That was enough.
- ✓ Print interviews. Every Sunday in the New York Times and many days in the Wall Street Journal, and other Journals in your local journals. You will see participants in my Coaching and Mentor Program cited in articles. They focus on approaching reporters and ensuring that reporters approach them.
- ✓ Articles. Determine what publications your buyers may be reading, and try to place your own articles there. Sometimes highly targeted newsletters are even better than major but more generic magazines.

- ✓ Columns. Once you have published articles successfully, pursue your contact with the goal of obtaining a regular column.
- ✓ Networking. Don't simplistically collect business cards. Find key buyers and recommenders, establish the beginnings of a relationship, offer them something of value, and follow up.

  Law: you have to give to get! (If you've found an executive recruiter who can recommend you to his clients, offer to recommend him to some people who need assistance hiring senior managers.)
- ✓ Pro bono work. If you find a cause you believe in that is nearby, offer to serve on a committee or task force (or, if it's possible, volunteer for the board). You'll find yourself surrounded by some significant buyers, recommenders, and influencers, who will perforce be your peers in the volunteer work. Nurture those relationships while doing good work.
- ✓ Newsletters. People complain to me that there are too many newsletters, but they don't understand the dynamics of competition. There are so many newsletters because people are reading them! (Remember Yogi Berra's dictum: "No one goes there any more, it's too crowded.") Competition opens markets. The keys to a newsletter are brevity (one computer screen), consistency (same time each month), and diversity (several short pieces instead of one "take it or leave it" piece).
- ✓ Blogs. There are 200 million blogs in the world as of this writing, and most of them are incredibly bad, to the point of being unreadable. However, those that stand out offer provocative ideas, controversy, intellectual property, and pragmatic help for the reader. Get a technical expert to run your blog, and

make sure that you use text, audio, and video to maximize the medium. (Make provision for video to go to YouTube, audio to go to iTunes, and so on. Archive everything on your blog.)
- ✓ Reach out. Contact trade association executive directors regularly, always offering value for the audience/membership. Ideally, provide a demo video.
- ✓ Broadcast media interviews. It's easier than ever to be interviewed on radio and TV (particularly if there is other gravity in place, such as a new book). You can record these and create marketing compilations, run them on your Web site, and so on.
- ✓ Community service. This is similar to pro bono, but it means serving on the planning board, school committee, parks commission, and so on. You'll find yourself quoted often in the press, and your background talked about.

Let me conclude by telling you what doesn't work and, worse, wastes your time, money, and repute:

- ✓ Paying to host a radio show. These are scams, appealing to the ego of the speaker, and you're usually paying to drone on to people who could not care less, while also having to bring on advertising! These are beyond stupid. (And paying to be on an infomercial with some doddering ex-C-list celebrity should be enough for your family to arrest you and place you in a home until you come to your senses. Only the people you pay for this travesty make any money from it.)
- ✓ Hosting your own cable TV show. These generally have the fake plants, tacky backdrop, rickety desk, and production values of a fourth-grade salute to the history of gerbils. When someone I've never heard of tells me that he or she is a "television show host,".
- ✓ Speaker "showcases" arranged by bureaus. No one is a buyer, no one is paying attention, and no one

- ✓ cares except the people who charged you to be at this swamp. These give vaudeville a good name.
- ✓ Direct mail and "cold calling." For every "expert" who claims that he or she knows how to book business doing this, I'll show you an "expert" who isn't a successful speaker but makes her money trying to teach people how to cold call. Would you hire a speaker in this manner? Do you buy stocks from the guys who call you with special offers at 8:30 at night? If so, you don't need this book, but you do need to send me all the money in your bank account as soon as you can put this down.
- ✓ Social media platforms. If you want to look for a job, peddle some offer to individuals, or keep track of old buddies, fine. Otherwise, this is one of the worst time dumps imaginable for true marketing of speaking services to corporate buyers. I've heard advocates say that social media "amplify" your message. The trouble is that they amplify all messages, regardless of their quality or relevance, into an incoherent cacophony.

Marketing is about creating need and emphatically demonstrating that you are the best person to fill that need. And it doesn't require staff, millions, or years.

SUMMARY

The Internet, like cable TV or fast food, can be a boon or a curse. Everything depends on how you utilize it.

Use your Web site as a credibility site, not a sales tool, because only low-level people and gatekeepers troll the Internet to find people. Senior-level buyers use references and referrals from peers, and may then go to your site to learn more about you (determine if you're a thought leader). Stop talking about credentials and initials that no one else understands, and start talking about typical client results.

If you find that you are in a position to work with bureaus, treat them as you would a client. Deal with the bureau principal, expect the bureau to market you in return for its 25 percent commission (don't pay more), require that funds be paid to you as received and not kept in escrow, and don't pay silly fees for "video reviews" or "marketing catalogs." Those are the bureau's cost of doing business, not yours.

You're better off focusing on trade associations, where you can get paid well to speak and speak in front of hundreds of buyers and recommenders.

To maximize your chances of success, use my Market Gravity approaches, starting with the ones that are most within your comfort zone, and then moving on to the others. That's how you'll become the center of attraction.

LEAN AND MEAN

WEALTH IS DISCRETIONARY TIME

One of my greatest discoveries is that wealth is about doing what you want when you want to. Wealth is discretionary time.

Time is not a resource issue, although many people think it is. We all receive a new 24 hours every day, rich or poor, young or old, sincere or passive-aggressive. We utilize it based on our priorities. Time is about assigning the correct amounts of time to the correct priorities. Running your speaking practice is about being lean and mean. Despite the somewhat mercenary title of this book, money is merely fuel for your life. If you work so hard and so long that you maximize your income no matter what, you may ironically be getting more money while you're actually eroding your wealth.

I can always make another dollar, but I can't make another minute.

LEAN AND MEAN SPEAKING PRACTICE

1. Outsource absolutely everything possible.

2. Do nothing other than what you must.

3. Use leveraged techniques.

4. Exploit technological and nontechnological shortcuts and advantages.

I'd never advise you not to have a staff. There are plenty of people who are highly successful explicitly because of hard-working, loyal, full-time staffers, and we'll examine those options momentarily. I'm simply suggesting that lean, mean, and green (money) can work quite well also, irrespective of the size of your practice. Give it some thought the next time you have a hiring itch. Don't set "automatic pilot" for the staff destination. Give it some thought because the money you spend on staff must be returned several times over through increased business, or it's money that you'll never see again.

In my estimation, less than 15 percent of successful speakers (that is, those who support their desired lifestyle through speaking and related activities) use full-time, paid staffs. So let's eliminate spouses and significant others, and let's place in abeyance for the moment those who are paid solely for performance, such as a marketer who earns a commission only on speeches sold for you.

ESSENTIAL AND LEGITIMATE STAFF CHARACTERISTICS

All right, let's assume that you need a staff because of the volume of your existing business or because of your understanding of your own marketing limitations or because all the kids on the block have one and you want one, too. Here are some criteria for staff acquisition.

Marketing Skills

At a minimum, the individual should be able to handle passive marketing, which generally consists of calls made to the office while you're not there. There's a huge difference between saying, "Mr. Weiss will get back to you" and saying, "What dates do you have in mind? What type of audience? It just so happens that Mr. Weiss is available on that date and has worked with those audiences as recently as last month. Would you like me to place a 'hold' on that date, and send you specific information and a sample contract?"

Ideally, the individual should have assertive marketing skills and should be able to find prospects, respond to leads, initiate cold calls, and determine which contacts can be closed without your help, which can be closed with your help, and which should be abandoned (or merely placed on a mailing list).

The individual should be able to identify and establish communication with the real buyer. Call these telemarketing skills.

Administrative Skills

The individual should be able to use standard office technology, including the creation of computer data banks; have keyboard skills and a professional phone manner; and handle the assembly of mailings, fulfilling of literature requests, product fulfillment, spreadsheet work, and travel scheduling.

If you have a staff, "shop" your own office, or have a colleague do it for you. Test to see how rapidly literature is mailed, how quickly leads are followed up and relayed, how a complaint is handled, and what general level of intelligence is conveyed about your practice.

Judgment

This person is representing you to the world, and the world will have much tougher expectations and standards than if they were leaving a message with automated equipment. People are funny that way. Consequently, your office help must return calls received in their absence promptly—within three hours at the outside. Complaints have to be assessed as valid ("You promised a press kit last week, and we haven't received it.") or invalid ("Why won't you send us a free copy of Mr. Weiss's materials so that we can evaluate them?").

Your staff members should be able to schedule your time and travel in full conformance with your preferences but without your active participation. They should be able to interact with colleagues, vendors, prospects, and clients professionally, articulately (after all, you do run a speaking business), and consistently with regard to your philosophy and manner.

Innovative Ability

One of the primary reasons to have assistance in this lonewolf profession is to get feedback and to challenge "the way we've always done it." Your staffer(s) should continually be able to recommend new, more efficient, and more productive methods to get results, ranging from mailings and new products to new speech topics and promotional literature. A staff person should know your business intimately, perhaps even better than you do, since he or she is watching it every day from a wide range of perspectives while you're preparing for the next speech and a new audience.

So the staff person should be someone whom you respect and trust, and to whom, you'll listen when new ideas are explored. If you find that new suggestions aren't regularly forthcoming or that you don't choose to engage in business discussions with the "administrative help," then you have the wrong resource. One of the results you're investing in a staff commitment is innovation and new ways to grow your practice.

Leverage

The investment in staff must result in leveraged growth on the profit line. If you're spending $45,000 a year on staff, enhanced revenues of $45,000 are woefully insufficient, and enhanced profit of $45,000 is breakeven. My advice is that your total outlay for staff resources ought to be returned three times over in profit or the investment isn't worth it. That's because, in addition to the tangible and measurable outlays, there are the intangible and immeasurable outlays of your time, attention, focus, and energy. Those of you who have managed people know exactly whereof I speak. Even with one person on board, there will be personal issues, training and education time, debate, confusion, and meetings. Multiply that accordingly by the size of the staff.

Hence, staff has to leverage your profit potential in any combination of these types of interventions:

- ✓ Acquisition of sales through aggressive cold calling and marketing
- ✓ Acquisition of sales through more rapid and effective lead follow-up
- ✓ Higher volume of mailings, client contacts, and responses
- ✓ Increased speaker sales and delivery time through less office time
- ✓ Improved visibility through increased interviews, articles, and so on
- ✓ More attractive offerings through new speech and product ideas

Let me state the obvious, in case you've missed it: if you are offsetting the bullet-point advantages through the investment of time required to manage, nurture, and otherwise tend to your staff, you are losing money hand over fist. You should be able to grow a successful practice by 10 to 15 percent a year simply through your own momentum and referral business, so a staff has to result in a 20 to 30 percent growth rate to make the investment worthwhile.

If a full-time staff can leverage your success, it's a wise and prudent investment. However, if you're not at that level or, like many of us, have reached that level and don't feel the need to invest in full-time resources, then contracting is always a wise choice.

Over the course of a year, I typically contract out for the following help related to my speaking business:

- ✓ Web and blog design and improvement
- ✓ Graphics creation
- ✓ Mailing fulfillment

- ✓ Mailing list maintenance
- ✓ Handout material creation
- ✓ Test and survey creation
- ✓ Product fulfillment
- ✓ Phone response (especially client "hot lines")
- ✓ Visual aids
- ✓ Audiovisual editing and dubbing
- ✓ Phone interviewing
- ✓ Newsletter formatting and proofing
- ✓ Material and product storage
- ✓ Travel arrangements

It often doesn't matter where subcontract help is located geographically these days since e-mail, fax, Skype, and FedEx can compensate handily for distance. Consequently, in my experience, the best ways to acquire contract help are

- ✓ Ask other speakers whom they use for what purposes.
- ✓ Ask other practitioners (lawyers, accountants, or consultants) whom they use for similar needs.
- ✓ Network through your local printer, Rotary, stationery supplier, or chamber of commerce.
- ✓ Place an ad for your needs in the local weekly newspaper.
- ✓ Post your need on the appropriate Internet bulletin boards.
- ✓ If you see something impressive, ask for the source (which is how I acquired my Web home page designer).
- ✓ Watch for ads in association newsletters (or place an ad yourself).
- ✓ Chat with neighbors who may be interested.
- ✓ Investigate local college work-study and intern offerings.
- ✓ Investigate local students seeking research projects.

Techniques for Professional, Honest Feedback

1. Recruit a mastermind group of people whose judgment you respect and who are familiar with the type of business you are in. These folks might include your financial planner, a colleague on a civic association, another entrepreneur (e.g., the person who owns one of your supply sources), a local politician or school board member, a business consultant, your attorney, and so on. They needn't be geographically proximate because this can easily be done via e-mail and computer.

Tell these people that you'll ask their help no more than two or three times a year. On those occasions, send them a tape (or invite them to hear you if you're speaking in their neighborhood) and ask them for their assessment of how you should reach the next level of the profession (larger audiences, larger companies, media work, high-visibility keynotes, and so on). Ask them what you do well, what should be further developed, and what underwhelms them, which might be abandoned. Don't react to stray comments, but if you see a pattern emerging, take action. (If one person says, "I didn't like that story," ignore it. But if five people say, "You seem to have no energy in those stories," then you know you've probably told them a few times too many.)

Guideline: Once is an accident, twice is a coincidence, three times is a pattern.

In return for their kindness, take your team out to dinner, offer to reciprocate for them, and/or provide a gift. You don't have to accept their advice, but you won't have it at all if you don't ask for it.

2. Seek out other speakers who are successful. Note that I didn't say "whom you like" or "whom you respect," because that leaves the door open for the mutual admiration society. There are a lot of speakers who don't make more than they do because they spend so much of their time telling each other how good they are and bestowing awards on each other.

Find exemplars who represent success with which you can

identify. Don't be taken in by the publicity klaxons wailing away. Everyone lives in an "oceanfront home," drives a "foreign car," and is "a prolific writer."

Find the time to develop relationships with those whom you see addressing the organizations you want to address in the capacity you want to assume. Or find someone with a platform presence that you admire, a visibility that impresses you, or a business acumen that you'd love to acquire.

Develop a network of several of these people whom you can access just a few times a year. Don't try to emulate their style or their attributes. Simply obtain frank feedback on your style, business, and direction that you can use to critically examine your progress. What's good for them might not be good for you, but their insights are from a highly valid frame of reference.

3. Invest in a formal mentoring relationship. There are some of us who are called upon so frequently for advice and guidance that the relationships have to take the form of formal consulting. In general, these relationships are focused and directed toward specific growth goals. You can stipulate what you want to tackle: penetrating the corporate market, using more humor, publishing, ancillary products, raising fees, and so on, and you can determine the duration. In my experience, you need at least six months of regular contacts with a mentor—which, again, needn't be in person—in order to create the follow-through and discipline to reach your goals.

The characteristics of a professional, effective mentor who will provide you with the proper ROI include

- ✓ Success as a speaker, not just as a mentor (a "doer," not an "expert")
- ✓ Unlimited access during the period, not designated days or times
- ✓ "Real time" help with actual prospects, fees, presentations, and so on

- ✓ Requirements for action and follow-up on those actions
- ✓ Contacts provided, such as book agents, speakers' bureau principals, and so on
- ✓ Solid references from other speakers

Mentors can be highly effective and well worth the investment if they can focus on your particular needs and offer specific, pragmatic techniques to grow your business and meet your personal objectives. Always eschew a "blanket" approach. This must be an individualized process.

4. Choose an association of professionals that is geared to provide feedback. At preliminary levels, Toastmasters International is a good alternative because it offers (predominantly amateur and/or infrequent) speakers the opportunity to hone their skills in front of a supportive audience. There are also contests run by the parent organization on local, regional, and national levels that provide the opportunity to perform in front of judges. The disadvantages of Toastmasters are that the feedback won't always be crisp and honest (I'm the next one up there, so I'm going to be kind) and that the criteria for speeches are narrow and somewhat inappropriate for corporate speaking.

5. Seek help on the Internet. There are numerous speakers' chat rooms, home pages, association listings, and similar sources. Allocate a morning to using the relevant search engines to generate alternatives. The beauty of the Internet is that you can exchange visual aids, speech transcripts, actual recordings, and online discussions if you have the proper equipment and software. On many sites, mine included, you can actually watch videos of keynotes and training sessions.

You're able, through cyberspace, to access a network of self-selected advisors who can provide you with downloadable examples of promotional literature, critiques of your speeches, advice on your business plans, opportunities internationally, and a host of other potentially useful feedback. If you're technologically able and individually willing, you can find a trove of help sitting right at your desk.

No matter what method you choose, find a source of direct and honest feedback: people who will tell you the truth and not simply stroke your ego. "Care more for the truth than what people think." Aristotle said that, and he wasn't a bad advisor.

SMALL PRINT: INCORPORATION, LEGAL, ACCOUNTING, INSURANCE, TAXES, YADA

Note, as always, that you should consult the proper insurance, legal, financial, and assorted other experts. However, make sure that they are also experienced in solo practices and in professional services firms. I'm not kidding; these are specialized fields, and you will otherwise get some awful advice.

Incorporation

By all means, incorporate your business, no matter what its size. (At this writing, Subchapter S and LLC are better bets than Chapter C, but the laws can change.) Do not listen to anyone who tells you that you don't have to incorporate.

Incorporation affords the following benefits and protection:

- ✓ A legal entity that can borrow money, sue, or be sued (so that your personal assets are safe—this is a litigious society)
- ✓ A professional status and sometimes a preferred status

—that is, as a small business—when seeking contracts or responding to RFPs (requests for proposals)
- ✓ Corporate benefits written into your bylaws, which may (consult your attorney) include a health plan, company car, and retirement plan; board of directors meetings; directors' fees; and other corporate amenities and perquisites
- ✓ Payment of all reasonable business expenses from before-tax funds
- ✓ Inclusion in certain lists and memberships restricted to corporate entities
- ✓ Favorable retirement plan options
- ✓ Favorable purchasing and health options

Incorporation can be accomplished painlessly by any competent, appropriate attorney for several hundred dollars or so, depending on your state's requirements.

Dr. Dennis Mulumba

Insurance

Aside from the basic lifestyle insurance that you should carry —health, life, dental, umbrella liability, whatever suits you— there are several other types that you should be absolutely certain to obtain:

1. Errors and omissions. This is typically called "E&O" in the insurance industry and "malpractice" by the rest of us. It protects you when you are being sued by a client for purportedly providing bad advice that has injured the client's firm. (Accidents such as someone tripping over your projector wire are covered by general liability insurance, which you should also carry; this is discussed next.) This type of suit has actually become more of a likelihood, given the increasing extent to which litigious remedies have replaced discussion and debate.

Theoretically, if you gave a speech on strategy that included warnings or opportunities for the audience, and the company acted on them and lost its corporate shirt, some legal beaver on the client's staff might advocate a suit against you. Consulting firms are being sued with increasing vigor, and a speaker's advice can be construed as consulting (and many of you are consultants, as well). Do not proceed in this business without E&O coverage. Do not pass "go." Do not collect your next fee without investing it in such protection.6

2. Liability insurance. If someone trips over your laptop power cord, that person will sue the conference facility, the computer manufacturer, the electric company, and YOU. This is the sad state of litigation these days. Liability insurance is cheap, is often provided by the same carrier that provides E&O coverage, and is a must.

3. Disability insurance. There is a far, far greater chance of our being disabled than of our dying during the most productive portions of our careers. Yet few speakers comprehend

the importance of disability coverage. Choose coverage that pays you for as long as you cannot return to your full and normal type of work (some coverage applies only as long as you can't be employed, irrespective of whether it's your normal type of work). The law and insurance company procedures usually dictate that you can carry total coverage equal to some percentage of your normal income, generally about 80 percent. As a speaker, you'll need to work with brokers or companies that are sensitive to the swings in potential income in this profession and can arrive at equitable average earnings in deciding about policy coverage amounts. As with any insurance, group plans are less expensive than individual plans, and a wide variety of trade associations—not necessarily speaking associations— offer the former with a variety of options (e.g., the longer the waiting period before the insurance kicks in, the less expensive the premium). You cannot afford not to have disability insurance, even if it means taking less life insurance for the moment.

4. Long-term care insurance. Usually referred to as "LTC," this provides for support and assistance at home when you are incapacitated for a long period, either now or in your elderly years. I mention it here because it is far cheaper to obtain when you are younger, and it provides the kind of financial support that can mean the difference between having to go to a nursing home and being cared for in your own home. I consider this coverage also to be a "must."

Financial Planning

For many speakers, financial planning means whatever is left after the checks are deposited and the bills are paid. That's not financial planning, but there is a name for it: bankruptcy.

It's silly and irresponsible to take the risks associated with an entrepreneurial business such as this one and not reap the rewards. While some of the rewards may be in instant gratification (especially for those of you from California), and you may feel that you can speak until you drop (and some people are apparently continuing to speak after they've dropped), you should have an intelligent long-term financial security plan.

Consult a first-rate financial planner (someone who charges a fee for the advice, not someone who earns a commission by selling you securities), set up a plan appropriate for your circumstances and objectives, and contribute to it faithfully, as though you're paying off the mortgage or the local utility. There are a variety of options and the laws change frequently, so keep abreast of what's best for you. Just one example: a SEP IRA, which is like a personal IRA, at the moment allows up to $47,000 a year to be contributed by your corporation, taxfree, to your retirement account. There are other goodies like this, so invest in professional help. You may also be able to set up 401(k) plans. The benefit of solo practice is that, while these plans often mandate that employees be covered, you have only yourself and perhaps a spouse to worry about.

Banking Relationships

My preference is to have a professional, as well as personal, relationship with a bank. Especially as your business grows and prospers, it makes sense to arrange for credit lines, references, advantageous interest rates, and all the other perquisites that remain hidden until, magically, they appear when you ask about them.

One other perk of this relationship: if you can become a "private banking customer" or whatever the euphemism is in your area, you can shortcut banking lines, obtain easy overdraft protection, and even have the bank cover an inadvertently unsupported check (or allow you to draw on uncollected funds). Banks do a lot for good customers that they obviously don't choose to advertise. If your bank is intractable about affording reasonable benefits, find another bank while saying a silent prayer for the competitive benefits of deregulation.

Motivational Summary

How many of you couldn't resist this heading? My final point is a simple but often ignored one: you are as successful as you position yourself to be.

As your business takes off, don't continue to regard it (or yourself) as the same enterprise it was when you received your first $500 check for speaking to the local trade association that couldn't find anyone else. The people who reach out to you usually want something—your dollars, your advice, your support, your repute. You have to reach out to make certain things happen on your terms. I'm astounded by the people who try to sell securities over the phone, since that seems to me to be the ultimate personal relationship business. But someone must be buying that way. Don't purchase insurance, vendor services, retirement plans, advice, or even pencils from just anyone who offers—and I'm someone who has seen speakers choose their attorney from the Yellow Pages of the phone book or an online experience on Facebook.

You're a success. Act like it. Choose your help carefully, but choose it now. The savvy of this business is in carving out your own route. Only the lead dog ever sees a change in scenery.

SUMMARY

You're a professional speaker, not a corporate manager. Your success is not a factor of how many people you hire; in fact, your success may be undermined by hiring a lot of people.

Lean and mean is the way to the green.

Above all, remember that true wealth is discretionary time. Speaking is a way to improve your life—you don't rearrange your life to enable your speaking. If you are happy and gratified only when you're in front of an audience, you need to seek help. If standing ovations and high "smile sheet" scores are your validation for occupying space on the planet, you have the depth of lawn clippings.

Be proud of your work, by all means, and be proud of your life, at all costs. Utilize subcontract and "virtual" support before you build infrastructure, which is not only expensive, but also very difficult to disassemble. Don't allow a corporate welfare state to build up around you. If you find you need constant adoration, get a dog.

Be careful about your corporate structure, bylaws, financial reporting, insurance, and related business needs. Maximize the use of pretax income. Don't let bureaus or tax authorities needlessly hold your money.

Be cautious about the people to whom you listen. Don't just speak like a pro. Listen like one, too.

SPEAKING MASTERY

COMMUNICATION BASICS

INTRODUCTION

The ability to send and receive information accurately and quickly on a daily basis is very vital in today's business environment- particularly for the entrepreneur. At work you are the face of the company and have to communicate with customers directly, whether face-to –face, over the phone, in writing or via the internet. You therefore have the power to influence customer behavior.

Today, information can be sent easily and quickly and whatever you do you are likely to be surrounded by documents and messages and expected to communicate regularly with colleagues, customers, suppliers, employees and others. The results of being a poor and inadequate communicator can range from minor difficulties to major business stress. Such is the importance of having proper business communication skills when you want to succeed in today's business world

UNIT OBJECTIVES

Upon completion of this unit you should be able to describe:

1. The elements of communication.

2. The process of communication.

3. The barrier to communication.

4. The importance of good communication skills.

TOPIC 1.1 – UNDERSTANDING COMMUNICATION

INTRODUCTION

Why do we communicate? To answer this question, we may need to ask ourselves and answer a series of questions. What do we mean when we say that communication has occurred? How do we know when we have effectively communicated? Can we send what we believe is a perfectly clear message and yet not be understood by those for whom the message is intended?

We communicate so that we can get our point across to the other people.

Communication is more than just the words that we speak; it is about how we express ourselves to other people and to the rest of the world. The purpose of Communication is to promote understanding, and this is done effectively via the two-way process that takes place when a message is sent through a medium and the receiver responds to the message by giving feedback. This feedback could either take the form of verbal or non-verbal feedback.

OBJECTIVES

Upon completion of this topic you will be able to:

1. Define communication.

2. Explain the communication process.

3. Employ the communication process.

WHAT IS COMMUNICATION?

Let us begin this topic by exploring your own personal definition of communication and why you think it is important.

Speaking Mastery

Make you notes below.

Activity – Personal Definitions

1. How would you define communications?

2. Do you think that communication is important in today's environment?

Record your answers to the questions in your personal journal. Record them as: Topic 1.1 Personal Definitions Answers.

Good Job! Now let's explore the definition of communication provided by other authors.

DEFINITION OF COMMUNICATION

Today communication has become difficult to define because it has come to mean practically anything. The word communication refers to the process by which we create and share meaning (Seiler, 2002). It is the act or process of giving or exchanging of information, signals, or messages either by talk, gestures, or writing.

Technically speaking, in the act of communication, we make opinions, feelings, information, etc known or understood by others through speech, writing or bodily movement.

(Taylor 2001) defines communication as giving, receiving or exchanging of information, opinions or ideas by writing, speech or visual means, so that material communicated is properly understood by everyone concerned.

Therefore we see communication as a process that involves the transmission and accurate replication of ideas, and is effective when it achieves the desired reaction or response from the recipient.

Now you may say that communication is important and that you spend most of your time doing it, and that you are pretty good at communicating. After all you talk to people, write notes, read books, get along with other people, and make you understood. So why should you study communication?

Dr. Dennis Mulumba

Just because we all communicate every day does not make us good communicators. Just because some aspects of effective communication are based on common sense does not mean common sense alone is enough.

Skilled communicators draw on an extensive and complex body of knowledge, including semantics (the study of word choice), linguistics (the study of language), rhetoric (the study of writing and speaking effectively), psychology, sociology, graphic design, and even computer science.

The ability to communicate is learned, and learning to be a competent communicator is a difficult, lifelong project. But you will make progress quickly if you work hard to learn the principles and concepts and then apply them in practice situations. (William J. Seiler, 2002)

Communication is critical to living successfully in today's society, but it is also important that you learn how to speak effectively, listen carefully and efficiently, think critically and be aware of and sensitive to differences in others. Then only will you be able to communicate effectively.

Remember:

• Communication is a process of sending and receiving verbal and nonverbal messages.

• Communication is considered effective when it achieves the desired reaction or response from the receiver.

• Communication is a two way process of exchanging ideas or information.

Activity - Let Us Take A Moment To Examine How We Communicate.

1. What happens when you talk?

2. What things might you talk about when you talk with:

a. A friend?

b. Your children?

c. A shopkeeper?

Speaking Mastery

d. Your brothers or sisters?

3. Do you think that you can communicate effectively without a purpose?

Record your answers in your course journal.

SO WHY DO WE COMMUNICATE?

The purpose of any given communication may be to:

1. initiate some action;

2. impart information, ideals attitudes, beliefs or feelings;

3. establish, acknowledge or maintain links or relations with other people

4. promote a product, service, or organization; and

5. relay information within the business; or deal with legal and similar issues.

At its most basic level, the purpose of communication in the workplace is to provide people with the information they need to do their jobs and to live their lives. In fact, communication is only successful when both the sender and the receiver understand the same information as a result of the communication.

The ability to communicate effectively with others is a top quality of a successful business person, however you may be a very intelligent person; but if you can't get your message across to others, you will be thought of as less intelligent than you are because ideas are common, but the ability to clearly communicate ideas to others is rare.

PRINCIPLES OF COMMUNICATION

To appreciate the true nature of communication, it is important to understand four fundamental principles:

• Communication is a process.

• Communication is both interactional and transactional.

• Communication can be intentional or unintentional.

• Communications happens in a context.

Communication is considered a process, because it involves a series of actions that has no beginning or end and is constantly changing (Berlo, 1960). It is like the weather that changes constantly and involves variables that can never be duplicated. Think about a relationship you developed with someone recently.

How did it occur? It may have happened by chance or it may have been a prearranged meeting. No two relationships are developed in the same way and no two communications are the same.

• The interactional and transactional aspects of communication are closely related. Interaction is an exchange of communication in which people take turns sending and receiving messages. An example of this is a phone conversation between two people. Transactional communication involves the sending (encoding) and receiving (decoding) of messages at the same time. An example of this is when you communicate with a family member. You not only send information but also receive information at the same time.

• Communications can occur regardless of whether it is intended or not.

When you communicate with others, you intend that that specific message be received. Intentional communication is a message that is purposely sent to a specific receiver. Unintentional communication is a message that was not intended to be sent or was not intended for the individual who received it.

• Communication cannot happen in a vacuum, there is always a setting or context in which the communication takes place. This context may be a location, a relationship or even a culture, for example waving to your best friend across a crowded room before an interview may be a way of saying "Good luck".

Activity – Communications Process

Now that we have provided a definition of communication, you should stop and think for a moment about the communication process. Respond to each of the following statements with either "True" or False. Give a brief explanation for your answer and record your response in your course journal.

1. Communication can solve all of our problems
2. The more we communicate the better
3. Communication is a natural ability
4. Communication is reversible

Adopted from (William J. Seiler, 2002) p6

In order to understand the complexity of this communication process you have to be familiar with the following terms referred to as elements:

ELEMENTS OF COMMUNICATION

There is no exhaustive list of the myriad components of communication; however the most basic elements are examined below.

• The process of communication has six components: sender/encoder, message, medium, receiver/decoder, and feedbacks.

Context

• Every message, whether oral or written, begins with context. Context is a broad field that includes country, culture, organization, and external and internal stimuli.

• Another aspect of context is the external stimuli.

• Internal stimuli have effect on how you translate ideas into a message.

• Your attitudes, opinions, emotions, past experiences, like and dislike education, job status and confidence.

Sender / Encoder

• While sending a message, you are the "encoder", the writer or speaker, depending on whether your message is written or oral.

• express your message so that the receiver(s)

• react as you desire

- You decide which symbols best convey your message and which message channel will be most effective among the oral and written media (letter, memo, telephone, etc)

Message

- The message is the main idea that you wish to communicate; it is of both verbal (written or spoken) symbols and nonverbal (unspoken) symbols. First decide exactly what your message is. Also consider the

receiver of your message.

Medium/Channel

- It means the way by which a message is communicated
- You can choose electronic mail, the printed word
- The choice of medium is affected by the relationship between the sender and the receiver.

Feedback

- Feedback can be oral or written; it can also be an action, such as receiving in the mail an item you ordered. Sometimes silence is used as feedback, though it is not very useful. Senders need feedback in order to determine the success or failure of the communication

NOTE: To communicate effectively it is important to limit the content of your message to a specific subject, and use this repeated back-and forth exchange to provide additional information or details in subsequent messages.

The figure below shows the key elements in the process of communication.

The communication process is not very complex. It consists of the elements mentioned above. The major players in the communications process are the sender and receiver.

Activity – The Communications Process – The Model

1. What do we call the following key players or elements in the

Speaking Mastery

communication process?

a. A person sending a message to another person.

b. The person for whom the message is intended.

c. An encoded set of verbal and non-verbal symbols.

2. Briefly explain the following elements of communication.

a. A message.

b. The messenger

c. The receiver.

d. Encoding.

e. Decoding.

3. Record your answers in your course journal.

Activity Responses

You must have identified the key players as follows:

1. Sender

2. Receiver

3. Message

4. Encoding

- A message: what needs to be communicated?

- A messenger: the person who has something to communicate.

- A receiver: the person who will receive the message.

- Encoding: verbal and non-verbal convention of communication.

- Decoding: reading by the receiver of the encoding done by the messenger.

COMMUNICATIONS TYPES USED TODAY

- Electronic Communication comprises different modes of communication out from the traditional way. It includes e-mail, fax, teleconferencing and voicemail. Electronic communication is used both internally and externally.

- Employment Communication is a mode of communication used for employees but specifically for accepting applicants for a job. It includes application letter, follow-up communications, interview and resumes.

- Nonverbal Communication is a mode of communication that uses body language and other means of communicating without the use of uttering words. It includes body language, expression, gestures, professional appearance, time or space.

- Verbal Communication is a mode of communication that uses the uttering of words in communicating to external contacts and employees. It includes feedback, instructions, presentations, and telephone.

- Written Communication is a mode of communication that requires writing in order to communicate. It includes letters, memos, proposals and reports.

Effective communication doesn't occur haphazardly in organisations. Nor does it happen all at once. Communication can be very complex, as there are countless opportunities for sending or receiving the wrong message.

Communication is a dynamic two-way process because the receiver then responds to the message (we call this giving feedback) and in this way he/she becomes the sender again, and the person who first spoke/wrote, becomes the receiver (of the feedback communication).

Activity – Personalized Communications Approach

Study the Communication Process illustrated earlier and the explanation of each of the element of the process. It is your turn now to draw your own communication model. Show prominently any three of

the elements which you find to be important for effective com-

Speaking Mastery

munication as an entrepreneur.

Record your diagram in your course journal.

Remember! It is important that all senders of communication must keep in mind who their target audience is, so that they can focus the message accordingly. The sender should know what the receiver's perception is, so that the encoding can be in line with the receiver's experiences. The sender should also use the appropriate communication channel to reach the receiver and invite feedback, so that they can confirm that the message was understood and appropriately responded to.

SUMMARY

It is important to remember that your communication needs to be clear and effective. Communication takes place when a message is sent in a specific code from the sender to the receiver through a medium, and the receiver responds to the message by giving feedback. The meaning of a message does not reside completely in the message. The receiver contributes meaning to this message when he or she interprets it in terms of his or her own background. If the message is not clear to the receiver this means that the

receiver may have interpreted the message differently from its intended purpose. If the receiver understood the message then he or she will provide positive feedback. Good feedback is essential in determining the effectiveness of the message.

BARRIERS TO COMMUNICATION

INTRODUCTION

Communication barriers can pop-up at every stage of the communication process (which consists of sender, message, channel, receiver, feedback and context –) and have the potential to create misunderstanding and confusion.

To be an effective communicator and to get your point across without misunderstanding and confusion, your goal should be to lessen the frequency of these barriers at each stage of this process with clear, concise, accurate, well-planned communications. This topic will focus on the different barriers to communication, and how those barriers can be overcome.

OBJECTIVES

Upon completion of this topic you will be able to:

1. Identify various barriers to communication.

2. Give some examples of the barriers to communication.

3. Suggest ways of overcoming these barriers.

COMMUNICATION BARRIERS

Pause for a moment and think about situations where you were unable to understand or convey an intended message.

Activity – Communications Breakdown

What do you think were the reasons for the breakdown in communication?

Take a minute to jot down your ideas in your course journal.

Communication will be incomplete and unsuccessful if you are unable to identify and understand the barriers of communication. These barriers are physical, sociological and psychological obstacles that interfere with the planning, organization, transmission and understanding of the message. There

are a number of such obstacles that can occur in the process of communication. The natural result of such obstacles or interfering factors is the misunderstanding of the message. These factors interfere with the self-confidence, self-disclosure and self-consciousness of the communication senders and receivers.

No matter how good the communication system in an organization is, unfortunately barriers can and do often occur. This may be caused by a number of factors which can usually be summarized as being due to:

- physical barriers,
- system design faults
- Additional barriers.

Communication barriers may be defined as factors that interfere with the effectiveness of the process of communication. When this process is interfered with the receiver does not understand the message, does not receive the message at all or decodes a distorted message. Barriers to communication are also referred to as 'noise', 'breakdowns', 'filters' or ' interference'. Barriers can occur at any point in the communication process and can be either internal or external

Figure 1. – Barriers to the Communication Process

NOISE

Noise hinders effective communication throughout the communication process. Noise can be from the external (surrounding) environment, such as from too many messages at the same time or background noise that interferes with a clear understanding of the message. We also refer to some receiver characteristics as 'noise', and this is where their emotions, ethnic background, age, education level or disabilities may distort or make a message misunderstood.

Noise in communication, is any distraction that interferes with the proper transmission of communication, so that the message from the sender cannot reach the receiver as it was intended by the sender to be understood. It is a major communication barrier, as we will see further on in this discussion. In tour guiding for example, noise can be the background sounds of animals at a sight while the tour guide is explaining the attractions. It could also be the accent of the person, which may make it difficult for another to understand the message he/she is trying to convey.

NOISE MAY FURTHER BE CLASSIFIED INTO TWO TYPES

Internal Noise – anything that distracts and distorts a communication without audible sound, for example the smell of a perfume when a person walks into the room or when the temperature in the room is too hot.

External Noise – anything that distracts and distorts a communication with audible sound for example the ringing of the cell phone or the pouring of the rain outside the house.

• Physical Barriers - are often due to the nature of the environment.

Any physical noise that disturbs the message so that it is not received properly can be seen as a physical barrier. Likewise, poor or outdated equipment, particularly the failure of management to introduce new

technology, may also be observed as a physical barrier. Distractions like background noise, poor lighting or an environment which is too hot or cold can all affect people's morale and concentration, which in turn interfere with effective communication.

• Semantic Barriers - A basic principle of communication is that the symbols the sender uses to communicate messages must have the same meaning in both the sender's and receiver's minds. You can

never be sure that the message in your mind will be clearly sent to your receiver.

System Design refers to problems with the structures or systems in place in an organization. Examples might include an organizational structure which is unclear and therefore makes it confusing to know who to communicate with. Other examples could be inefficient or inappropriate information

systems, a lack of supervision or training, and a lack of clarity in roles and responsibilities which can lead to staff being uncertain about what is expected of them.

Attitudinal Barriers come about as a result of problems with staff in an organization. These may be brought about, for example, by such factors as poor management, lack of consultation with employees, personality conflicts which can result in people delaying or refusing to communicate, the personal attitudes of individual employees which may be due to lack of motivation or dissatisfaction at work, brought about by insufficient training to enable them to carry out particular tasks, or just resistance to change due to entrenched attitudes and ideas.

• Physiological Barriers – These are barriers that result from the state of condition of the body. For example, the working conditions that affect our health or the impairment of the sensory organs. Our health gets affected by poor working conditions, poor working designs within the organization as well as poor lighting. Persons who are impaired have unavoidable barriers in their communication, however for most the impairment does not prevent them for communicating effectively.

• Psychological Barriers – referred to an individual's state of mind. If a person has been disturbed at some point, they are most likely not going to concentrate on a message. The psychological barrier that

disturbs communication may be referred to as either psychological noise – any emotion mannerism or attitude that causes the message to be affected negatively. For example if a student received poor

grades in a communication examination they may be too upset to pay attention to the teacher in the class. Sometimes this limitation may cause an emotional outburst.

Stereotyping

Stereotyping is an image idea or character that has become fixed, unchanged and standardized in the conventional form without permitting or encouraging actual individual differences. When we single out one attribute that a person has which is normally negative and ignore the rest of their good characteristics or positive characteristics we would be stereotyping that individual.

If we form negative stereotypes of people we communicate with, it may affect our communication with them. If we stereotype people and structure in our message, in a negative way we might inadvertently offend people, especially the persons who do not conform to any particular stereotype.

MENTAL AND EMOTIONAL BARRIERS

Your mental or emotional state as well as those of your visitors may also affect the way in which a message is conveyed or interpreted. Consider the following examples:

• Emotional stress, anger, depression or sadness during the communication process. Such negative emotions may influence how you send the message and in turn may block the message in the mind of the receiver. This results in a message that is not clearly understood.

• Too much or too little information or information that is inaccurate. If you fail to prepare and do the necessary research you may lack confidence and questions may exceed your personal knowledge. These too are barriers to effective communication.

• A distorted and subjective focus in your commentary.

For example: expressing your personal political, ethnic or religious views.

• Insecurity or a lack of confidence may also be a major barrier to effective communication.

• Difficult personalities you may encounter. Some tourists may be aggressive and may have exaggerated demands while others may be passive. Such situations may create barriers to effective communication.

Activity – Personal Reflection

Based on the barriers discussed in the above sections, share any personal experience you have had where you were unable to send an intended message.

Record your response in your course journal.

Activity – Communications Problems

Review the cartoon above and then answer the following questions.

1. Identify the problem with which the receptionist was initially confronted.

2. What caused the communications problem?

3. What could have happened because of this problem?

Record your answers in your course journal.

OVERCOMING BARRIERS TO COMMUNICATION

Everybody at some stage experiences communication breakdown, where the message is not received as the sender intended. There are also many ways of overcoming such limitations however, the following section will help us understand those limitations so as to ensure smooth and effective communication of message.

- Use of Simple Language: Use of simple and clear words should be emphasized.

Use of ambiguous words and jargons should be avoided.

- Reduction and elimination of noise levels: Noise is the main communication barrier which must be overcome on priority basis. It is essential to identify the source of noise and then eliminate that source.

- Active Listening: Listen attentively and carefully. There is a difference between "listening" and "hearing". Active listening means hearing with proper understanding of the message that is heard. By asking questions the speaker can ensure whether his/her message is understood or not by the receiver in the same terms as intended by the speaker.

- Emotional State: During communication one should make effective use of body language.

He/she should not show their emotions while communication as the receiver might misinterpret the message being delivered. For example, if the conveyer of the message is in a bad mood then the receiver might think that the information being delivered is not good.

• Avoid Information Overload: The managers should know how to prioritize their work. They should not overload themselves with the work. They should spend quality time with their subordinates and should listen to their problems and feedbacks actively.

• Give Constructive Feedback: Avoid giving negative feedback. The contents of the feedback might be negative, but it should be delivered constructively.

Constructive feedback will lead to effective communication between the superior and subordinate.

• Proper Media Selection: the medium through which communication passes should be properly selected. Simple messages should be conveyed orally, like: face to face interaction or meetings.

Use of written means of communication should be encouraged for delivering complex messages.

For significant messages reminders can be given by using written means of communication such as: Memos, Notices etc.

• Flexibility in meeting the targets: For effective communication it is important to ensure that the individuals are meeting their targets timely without skipping the formal channels of communication.

Activity - Perception

Can you describe what you see in this picture?

Take another look at the picture; is it an old lady or a young lady you thought you saw in the figure?

What do you think was the intention of the communicator/artist who drew this picture?

Show this picture to three other persons and see what they perceive.

Speaking Mastery

Record your responses in your course journal.

Response to Activity 1.2D

1. Did your description included words similar to old or witch-like or hag?

2. Or did your description included words similar to young or beautiful or elegant or well dressed?.

3. Look again at the picture. You should be able to see both a young and an old lady.

(If you cannot see both the young and the old lady, ask your tutor to point both out to you.)

4. Was it an old lady or a young lady that you were intended to see?

5. Do you see what was intended to be communicated to you or did you see something else?.......

SUMMARY

The barriers of communication are dangers to any organization if they are not removed on time. When the communicator transmits the idea in an unchanged and undistorted form to the receiver and the receiver responds to it, then, the process of the communication is supposed to have been perfect.

But this process of 'perfect' communication can never exist due to the number of factors, which stand in its way as the barriers. The communicator has to identify and understand the reasons for poor communication in order to communicate effectively. Understanding the process of communication is the first step towards improving the abilities and skills of communication, but understanding the factors that prevent us in transmitting the exact meaning is very essential for effective communication.

TOPIC 1.3 – TYPES OF COMMUNICATION

Dr. Dennis Mulumba

INTRODUCTION

In the previous topic, we took a look at the barriers to communication. These barriers may be eliminated when one is aware of the different types and forms of communication present today. Did you know that there are other types of communication other than oral and written communication?

In this topic we will examine the different types and forms of communication with special emphasis to non-verbal communication.

OBJECTIVES

Upon completion of this unit you will be able to:

1. Identify the different types and levels of communications in the workplace.

2. Explain the systems of communication.

3. Discuss the different forms of communication.

TYPES OF COMMUNICATION

The type of communication is usually distinguished by the number of people involved in the communication, the purpose of the communication, and by the degree of formality in which it occurs.

When you communicate you interact and react. You exchange information, ideas, plans, and make decisions, rules, proposals, contracts, and agreements.

All these activities require one skill that is communication. So we can say that communication is the "Lifeline" of every person or organization and for you to exchange information within and outside the organization or with other people you need to use a variety of formal and informal forms of communication that carry the flow of information.

Four types of communication are discussed below: intrapersonal, interpersonal, small group and team, and public.

• Intrapersonal Communication – to communicate with others you must first understand how you communicate with yourself. The process of understanding information within oneself is called intrapersonal communication.

As we grow we learn alto about ourselves and our surroundings and much of what we learn is gained from our own experiences. Intra personal communication includes internal activities such as thinking, problem solving, evaluating, emotions and stress. All messages that we create first occur within us.

This makes communication a personal event. Intrapersonal communication may occur without the presence of any other type of communication, but all other types of communication cannot occur without it.

• Interpersonal Communication –the informal exchange of information between two or more people is referred to as interpersonal communication; it includes informal conversations such as talks with parents, friends, children, acquaintances or strangers as well as more formal conversations such as an Interview.

• Small Group Communication - A subcomponent of interpersonal communication - small-group communication, is an exchange of information among a relatively small number of persons who share a

common purpose.

• Public Communication - a message is transmitted from one person to a number of individuals who listen. The most widely used form of public communication is the public speech.

COMMUNICATION SYSTEMS

For communication to be considered effective, you need to know how to keep the communication routes open. What follows is a simple discussion on the communication systems that may be used in different settings:

Downward Communication

Organizational decisions are made at top level and then flow down to the people who carry them.

When employees receive appropriate downward communication from the management, they become

motivated and more efficient. Downward communication frequently makes use of communications like memos, notices, in-house newsletters, handbooks and procedure manuals.

Upward Communication

The upward communication flow is equally important as downward communication. Communications are directed upward to managers or supervisors by using memos, reports, meetings and informal discussions. Successful managers listen closely to opinions, complaints, problems, and suggestions, especially when these are clearly put forward.

Horizontal Communication

Horizontal communication occurs between people of the same status – departmental heads, directors, supervisors or between peers in organizations in order to solve problems, performs job duties, prepare for meetings, and cooperate on important projects.

Internal Communication - This communication takes place within the

organization and falls under two categories:

• Internal oral communication which includes telephone, face-to-face

discussions, intercom, presentation, meetings and conferences.

• Internal written communication which includes memos, reports,

graphs/charts, email, fax, notices, minutes, newsletters etc.

Informal Internal Communication - Every organization has an informal communication network – a grapevine: this term describes an unofficial

communication system which is constantly changing. It is an important source

of casual conversation. However it may be viewed as vehicle for distortions of

the truth, rumor or gossip.

Figure – Internal Oral Communication

EXTERNAL COMMUNICATION

Communication that takes place outside the organization is called external

communication and falls under two categories:

- External oral communication- which includes meetings, conferences/

seminars, conversations, telephone communication and presentations

- External written communication – which includes advertisements,

notices, reports, emails, fax, letter, invitations, leaflets/brochures,

forms/ questionnaires etc

TELEPHONE

MEETINGS

PRESENTATIONS

FACE-TO-FACE

MESSAGES

INTERCOM

ORAL

Forms of Communications

List the different forms of communications explained above that you have personally used during your career and briefly describe how you used them?

Who was the receiver? What was the message? What was the response?

Record your observations in your course journal.

FORMS OF COMMUNICATION

Communication involves the exchange of information in the form of messages, signs, symbols and thought. This exchange of information can be relayed to the sender through different forms, three of which will be discussed below:

• Oral Communication: Oral communication refers to the spoken words in the communication process. Oral communication is information spoken by mouth; the use of speech.

Some of the examples of Oral Communication are: Face to face communication, Telephonic Communication, Public Address System (Speech), Informal rumor mill (Grape Wine), Audio & Visual Media(Radio, TV), Lectures, Conference- Interchange of views, Meetings, Cultural Affairs.

• Written Communication: Communication by means of written symbols (either printed or handwritten).

Some of the examples are:

- Orders,
- Instructions,
- Letters,
- Memos,
- Reports,
- Policy manuals,
- Information Bulletin,
- Complaint System,

- Suggestion System, etc.

The effectiveness of the written communication will depend on the style of writing and also the clarity and precision of language.

Graph

News Letter

Brochure

Leaflets

Forms

Charts

Invitations

Notices

Report

Email

Fax

Letter

WRITTEN

• Non-Verbal Communication - is the overall body language that a person uses when they engage in communication.

These include body posture, hand gestures, facial expressions and the overall body movements.

Non-verbal communication is also known as SEMIOLOGY (communication that does not use words). Facial expressions form a major part of non-verbal communication because it communicates instant expression about a person's mood.

This does not mean that other non-verbal elements are not equally important. A firm handshake can independently express emotion as well.

Non-verbal communication can also be observed in the form of signboards, photographs, sketches or even paintings. Most of the time we consciously and unconsciously use the elements of non-verbal communication to support the verbal messages that enhance our communication's. In other words, effective two way communication depends on our ability to interpret non-verbal signs.

Table - Classification of Non- verbal Communications

Classification Description

Proximics: Examines individual personal space. It takes into account body spacing and postures.

The physical distance between two people can suggest whether the relationship is a personal on or a business one.

- Intimate distance- embracing, touching or whispering

- Personal distance – interaction among friends

- Social distance- interaction with formal acquaintances, colleagues, business persons

- Public distance – interaction with strangers and also during public speaking.

Chronemics: Usage of time – communication may be expressed through punctuality, willingness to wait for something, speed of speech or even the time people are willing to listen to each other.

Classification Description

Kinesics: Body movements, facial expression and gestures and will include:

- Posture - how you sit, and how you lean forward communicate information about you

• Gestures – they allow us to express a variety of emotions and thoughts like contempt, hostility or affection.

Haptics: Touching as a tool of non-verbal communication, eg, a firm handshake or a pat on the back. The meaning conveyed by a touch will depend on other factors also like context as well as situation or even the relationship between two individuals.

Oculesics: Expressions communicated through the eyes. Eg a glance or a gaze or even the blinking of the eyes

Paralanguage/Vocalics: Non- verbal cues of the voice which include, Pitch, tone, volume, tempo, rhythm:

• Vocal characterizers: laughing, crying, sighing, yawning, clearing the throat, groaning, yelling, whispering.

• Vocal Qualifiers: intensity (loud/soft); pitch height (high/low).

• Vocal Segregates: sounds such a 'uh-huh', 'um', 'uh'; silent pauses.

Classification Description

Environmental

Factors

The environment can influence the outcome of communication. For this reason, you have to give careful consideration to office space, factory layout, the sales area and conference venues.

The environment should put people at ease and match their expectations; an unsuitable environment can produce 'noise' that causes communication barriers and interferes with the communication process.

In the workplace, attention to punctuality or a disregard for it can make a strong nonverbal impact.

A disregard for punctuality may, like a sloppy appearance, merely reflect a casual attitude. However, a deliberate decision to keep a contact waiting may be a way to communicate a negative message.

Artifacts: Artifacts are objects used to convey nonverbal messages about self-concept, image, mood, feeling or style.

For example, perfume, clothes, lipstick, glasses and hairpieces project the style or mood of the wearer.

Many artifacts are common to the group but we also use artifacts, particularly clothing, as an individual form of communication.

COMMUNICATIONS ACCORDING TO STYLE AND PURPOSE

Formal Communication - This includes all the instances when communication has to take place in a formal format – the style is formal and in most cases very official. Business meetings, official conferences would make use of official letters and memos to convey their message.

Formal communication is straight forward, it is to the point and has a rigid tone to.

Informal Communication - this includes instances where people share a casual dialogue or conversation with each other.

There are no strict guidelines to follow. They do not necessarily have boundaries of time like formal communication. This type of communication occurs between friends or persons who have a very good relationship.

Interpretation

Look at the picture above:

1. What type of communication is taking place in the picture above?

2. Examine the different types of communication that are featured under non-verbal communication. How will the person's

Speaking Mastery

expression change if placed in all the situations of non-verbal communication?

Record your observations in your course journal.

SUMMARY

In this topic we examined the different types of communication that you can use to get your message across effectively.

Communication, whether oral or written is all about understanding. Effective communication can be achieved by having thorough knowledge of the communication cycle, being aware of the barriers which may exist and by carefully considering the following vital factors:

• What is the objective of the communication? is it intended to give information, to persuade, to request, to inform

• Who will receive that information?

• Under which circumstance is the communication taking place?

• How will the recipient react to the communication?

COMMUNICATIONS SKILLS

INTRODUCTION

Communicating with others is an essential skill in our ever growing business environment. Do you often find yourself misunderstanding others? Do you have difficulty getting your point across clearly? When it comes to communication, what you say and what you don't say are equally important.

OBJECTIVES

Upon completion of this topic you will be able to:

1. Identify good communication skills.

2. Understand the importance of communication skills.

3. Identify the benefits of effective communication.

COMMUNICATION SKILLS

Good communication skills are skills that facilitate people to communicate effectively with one another. Effectual communication engages the choice of the best communications channel, the technical know-how to use the channel, the presentation of information to the target audience, and the skill to understand responses received from others.

Self-development, interpersonal skills, mutual understanding, mutual cooperation and trust are also important to set a complete channel of most effective and winning communication skills.

Interpersonal communication skills-Simply put interpersonal skills are the skills we use to interact or deal with others. Interpersonal skills are sometimes also referred to as communication skills, people skills and/or soft skills.

How we deal with others can greatly influence our professional and personal lives, improving these skills builds confidence and enhances our relationships with others Interpersonal communication is the process by which people exchange information, feelings and meaning through verbal and non-verbal

messages.

This definition highlights the important fact that interpersonal communication is not only concerned with what is said, i.e., the language used, but how it is said, e.g. the non-verbal messages

sent, such as tone of voice and facial expressions.

Speaking Skills – most people find talking easier than writing because it is not so complex and because phrases can be used in speech which would be unacceptable in written communication.

However, if communication is to be effective oral communica-

Speaking Mastery

tion should be planned just as carefully as planning what you write. Given below are some guidelines that you may use to create a well-structured oral message

- Decide what your message is

- Identify the key points in your message

- Choose an appropriate style to convey your message

- When delivering the message, monitor feedback constantly

- Know when you have said enough and try to end on a positive note

Expressive Skills - are required to convey message to others through words, facial expressions and body language -

Listening Skills - are skills that are used to obtain messages or information from others. Listening is half of oral communication, and it is a skill that needs to be practices and taken equally as seriously as speaking. Here are some guidelines to follow if you want to be an effective listener:

- Prepare to listen – concentrate on what is being said, learn to listen, not just hear

- Avoid pre-judgement – do not just to conclusions before hearing what is said

- Be open-minded – hear what is said and not what you would like to hear

- Establish eye contact

- Watch for signals - pick up aspects that the speaker considers important by watching posture and gestures and listening to intonation in the speakers words

- Extract the main points – pick out the key words and phrases

- Give feedback – learn to give positive feedback and ask questions to assist your understanding of the message

- Make notes – record important information that can be used as a reminder of the communication

The importance of good communication skills can never be ignored or neglected.

With good communication skills, you can have a team of members who together create an ambience of open communication, concise messages, probe for clarifications, recognize nonverbal signals, and mutual understanding.

Good communication skills are an invaluable asset to everyone.

While the importance of verbal communication cannot be underestimated, one cannot do away or ignore written communication. A simple billboard, carrying a well written message, manages to hold our attention at a crossing while authors have been mesmerizing voracious readers by the power of their words.

The enthralled reader flips through the pages, reading well into the night, without giving much thought to the mode of communication. The above examples clearly illustrate the importance of communication skills.

Interpersonal Communications

When you have the opportunity to observe interpersonal communication, make a mental note of the behaviours used, both verbal and non-verbal.

If this is not possible, you could examine some of the different ways interpersonal relationships are conveyed on the television. Make notes about your observations in your course journal on the following:

1. Who are the communicators?

2. What messages were exchanged?

3. What (if any) noise distorts the message?

4. How is feedback given?

5. What is the context of the communication?

WHY ARE COMMUNICATION SKILLS ESSENTIAL?

In any form of business, communication is an internal as well as an external affair.

The success of the business rests upon communication and it has become all the more essential due to the following reasons:

1. Mutual co-operation: People have to perform different tasks. Sound communication is essential for ensuring mutual co-operation and understanding between people.

2. Technological advancements: Rapid changes in science and technology lead to obsolescence of technology and knowledge. In order to upgrade technology, entrepreneurs must persuade their employees to accept new technology. Regular communication becomes necessary to update knowledge and to provide the skills needed to apply new technology.

3. Competition: Liberalization and globalization have resulted in severe competition between and within business. Persuasive communication in the form of advertisements, personal contacts and publicity becomes essential to survive in the race of competition.

4. Trade union movement: In all sectors, employee unions are very strong and powerful.

Managers must consult union leaders on several matters.

The exchange of information and ideas between entrepreneurs and union officials helps to maintain healthy relations between them.

5. Human relations: Effective communication is necessary to develop mutual trust and confidence. Participation in the decision-making process and other means of communication help to develop a sense of belonging and loyalty.

6. Public relations: Society expects more and more from its members in organizations.

Entrepreneurs and managers have to keep Government, distributors, suppliers, investors and other sections of society well-informed about their contributions to society.

Public relations help to improve image in society and big enterprises employ professional experts for this purpose.

7. Personal asset: Communication skill is essential for success in every job.

Entrepreneurs and Managers are required to deliver speeches, write documents and conduct interviews. The ability to communicate effectively is equally essential for promotion in career.

Good communication is the foundation of good business and entrepreneurial skills. It is essential not only for the growth and success of the business but also for personal growth.

However, just theoretical knowledge is not enough. If an entrepreneur does not possess practical communication skills, he/she would fail. The entrepreneur may have all the requisite technical skills, know the business and policies but fail to communicate effectively.

This inadequacy overshadows the other skills.

Generally, the main problem is that the effort to communicate is missing.

Good communication is an essential skill in being personally effective. It is also an essential skill for everyone who works for supervisors and managers or who is part of a team at work, home or socially. How often have you felt that someone doesn't understand, that they take you for granted, that you're not taken seriously, that people twist what you're saying, that your rights have been ignored, angry that you can't express yourself at the time.

Most of us will have felt at least some of these at some time or another.

You may react by getting angry or aggressive, or by avoiding situations that cause conflict and pain, or by agreeing to things because you feel powerless and want a quiet life.

All of these activities are based around establishing and maintaining good methods of communication. However, your ability to communicate effectively will be governed by many things, but mainly on your development of skills which will help you to balance the interests, rights and reactions of others with our own.

GUIDELINES TO EFFECTIVE COMMUNICATION

The list of communication skills presented below may be used as a guideline while interacting with others:

- Staying focused while communicating is very important.

Concentrating hard, should help in catching the speaker's views and responding to them with ease.

- Developing effective listening skills is as important as speaking during a communication process. Good listeners don't have to spend much time in understanding what the other person has to say. However one can also respond in a much more precise manner, if the whole thing is understood quickly. Feedback given by good listeners reduces the effort of speakers to elaborate on things to be communicated.

- Making eye contact while speaking/and listening is a way to assure the other person that you are following the communication process with interest. Looking away from the speaker or just not concentrating, can exhibit your poor communication skills.

- The aspect of body language should be given as much importance as verbal communication while interacting with people. It is one of the main components in the list of interpersonal skills. An open stance indicates that a person is interested in communication.

- Attitude of the speaker holds great importance while communicating.

Listening to the speaker patiently and then keeping forth our views should be the right thing to do. The attempt should not be that of winning over an argument.

- Speaking clearly is again an important thing to keep in mind.

Merely pronouncing the words clearly is not enough. The other person should be able to understand our views/thoughts clearly. Any kind of ambiguity leads to confusion.

• One should not use harsh language even if he/she finds the opponent's views to be conflicting with his/her opinion. Disagreeing or keeping forth our disapproval about a particular thing in a polite way

is possible. Once again, patience is the key to handle such situations.

BENEFITS AND IMPORTANCE OF EFFECTIVE COMMUNICATION

The ability to communicate effectively is necessary in todays fast past environment. The importance of speech and words whether through voice or a paper is a communication medium to convey information and direction.

Without communication there is no way that we would be able to express thoughts, expressions and ideas.

The lack of effective communications may lead to:

• Misunderstandings.

• Lack of information.

• Decrease in employees' performance.

• Increase in company's turnover, as a result.

Ineffective or poor communication is frustrating and becomes a source of a conflict. The inability to clearly express thoughts, ideas and demands leads to an individual's inability to perform work well. Such a situation may take place when an employee is not truly aware of what is requested of them.

This decreases the satisfaction an employee gets from the job.

• If a manager is able to communicate his/her ideas clearly, so that employees definitely know what is asked of them, the subordinates will, consequently, perform their jobs correspondingly.

Speaking Mastery

On contrast, an aggressive way of managing reports results in employees' getting more and more frustrated, often guessing what their real faults

• A good style of entrepreneurship, as well as a positive approach to communication, ensures that the entrepreneur and the employee understand each other, and are more effective at the workplace

• Effective communication provides individuals with a clear understanding of what is demanded from them, with knowledge of what to do and what to expect.

• Effective communication can be done using various internal journals, magazines, pamphlets and intranet. They can serve as official proof of the happening of an event and other information.

• Effective listening and trusting the speaker are two essential elements which help people concentrate on the subject matter of communication.

While communicating, all people should keep the objectives of communication in mind and avoid any bias towards each other.

• Communication establishes a bond among people and effective communication helps people save their precious time and increase personal and professional productivity.

• Attempts should be made to seek feedback from the receivers of information to ensure that communication has actually taken place.

Without a proper feedback, the process of effective communication is incomplete.

• Communication helps people understand what is expected of them and how to convert their talent into performance

• Effective communication reduces the chances of mistakes and misunderstandings. When there is greater and more effective interaction between persons there will be lesser number of mistakes and misunderstandings.

To achieve the desired standard of communication, constant

efforts are required. Any failure in the communication results in chaos and defeated purposes.

Proper flow of communication ensures harmony among all individuals.

Persons who have developed effective communication skills are able to:

• Listen attentively and empathically, enabling them to minimize and resolve conflict, resulting in less frustration and stress.

• Form and maintain good interpersonal relationships at all levels, creating better co-operation between people.

• Form and maintain good relations with external publics.

• Speak effectively, thereby being able to provide and exchange information and give sensible feedback.

• Motivate and encourage people to be more productive in reaching specific goals.

• Consider problems logically, make decisions about what they think and therefore solve problems effectively.

• Persuade colleagues to think the way they do, increasing effective team work and group discussion.

• Save time and money.

People with good communication skills are very successful in motivating others and therefore tend to lead people in a desired direction efficiently.

Good business communication leads to enhanced leadership skills.

SUMMARY

It can take a lot of effort to communicate effectively. In this lesson you examined the different skills that you could use to make your communication more effective. However, you need to be able to communicate well if you're going to make the most of the opportunities that life has to offer.

Good communication is essential not only for the growth and success of the business but also for personal growth. However, just theoretical knowledge is not enough. If you do not possess practical communication skills, you will fail to communicate effectively.

Good communication is an essential skill in being personally effective. How often have you felt that someone doesn't understand, that they take you for granted, that you're not taken seriously, that people twist what you're saying, that your rights have been ignored, angry that you can't express yourself at the time. Most of us will have felt at least some of these at some time or another.

You may react by getting angry or aggressive, or by avoiding situations that cause conflict and pain, or by agreeing to things because you feel powerless and want a quiet life.

All of these activities are based around establishing and maintaining good methods of communication. However, your ability to communicate effectively will be governed by many things, but mainly on your

development of skills which will help you to balance the interests, rights and reactions of others with your own.

Self-Reflection:

By learning the skills you need to communicate effectively, you can learn how to communicate your ideas clearly and effectively, and understand much more of the information that's conveyed to you.

As either a speaker or a listener, or as a writer or a reader, you're responsibility is to make sure that the message is communicated accurately.

Pay attention to words and actions, ask questions, and watch body language.

These will all help you ensure that you say what you mean, and hear what is intended.

UNIT SUMMARY

In this unit we explored the communications process and how to ensure your personal and professional messages are received and interpreted correctly.

Business is marketing and innovation as well as communications.

Effective communications will support the marketing and sales process and ensure that products and services are provided to the customer in a timely fashion.

Ineffective or poor communications will result in lost productivity, poor employee morale, unsatisfied customers and potential failure of the business.

During the remainder of this course you will be provided guidelines on how to improve your business communications process.

But before you move on to the next unit you should complete the unit assignment described below.

UNIT ASSIGNMENT

Answer all the questions and record your answers in a Word document that can be forwarded to your instructor.

1. What is your definition of communication?

2. Can you identify the main elements of communication in the model above?

3. Explain the function of each of the elements identified in the model above.

4. Describe a message that you would like to send to a group of persons and explain it using the model above.

5. Below is correspondence that was sent to workers regarding the Total Eclipse of the sun. The correspondence was sent from the managing director to his executive director who in turn

communicated it to the departmental heads in the business.

Read the series of messages and identify any barriers that are present.

Did the message change as it was being forwarded by each level in the chain of command?

From: Managing Director

To: Executive Director

'Tomorrow morning there will be a total eclipse of the sun at nine o'clock. This is something which we cannot see every day.

So let the work-force line up outside, in their best clothes to watch it. To mark the occasion of this rare occurrence, I will personally explain the phenomenon to them. If it is raining we will not be able to see it very well and in that case the work force should assemble in the canteen.'

From: Executive Director

To: Departmental Head

'By order of the Managing Director, there will be a total eclipse of the sun at nine o' clock tomorrow morning. If it is raining we will not be able to see it in our best clothes, on the site.

In this case the disappearance of the sun will be followed through in the canteen. This is something we cannot see happening every day.'

From: Departmental Heads

To: Sectional Heads

'By order of the Managing Director, we shall follow the disappearance of the sun in our best clothes, in the canteen at nine o'clock tomorrow morning.

The Managing Director will tell 15 of us whether it is going to rain. This is something which we cannot see happen every day.'

From: Section Heads

Dr. Dennis Mulumba

To: Foreman

'If it is raining in the canteen tomorrow morning, which is something that we cannot see happen every day, the Managing director in his best clothes, will disappear at nine o' clock.'

From: Foreman

To: All Operators

'Tomorrow morning at nine o' clock, the Managing Director will disappear. It's a pity that we can't see this happen every day.

Adopted from

http://v5.books.elsevier.com/bookscat/samples/9780080465296/9780080465296.pdf

List the barriers to each message and how they were mis-interpreted.

Instructions

Once you have answered all of the questions and completed this exercise submit it to your instructor for review, feedback and grading.

PRESENTATION SKILLS

INTRODUCTION

At times a professional must produce and deliver a formal presentation often supported by PowerPoint or some other visual media.

The effectiveness of the presentation is measured by the audience response.

Speaking Mastery

Depending on the propose of the presentation this response could be in the form of a commitment to your products and services; increased sales; support from your stakeholders; etc.

Mastering the art of presentation is not always an easy task, especially for those who struggle with public speaking. This topic will explore the art of formal presentations and provide guidance on how to effectively deliver the information to your audience.

OBJECTIVES

Upon completion of this topic you will be able to:

1. Analyze your target audience for a formal presentation.

2. Produce content appropriate for the target audience.

3. Effectively employ visual aids.

4. Confidently deliver a formal presentation.

STEPS IN PRODUCING A FORMAL PRESENTATION

There are five phases in the preparation of formal presentations. Each of the five phases is summarized below, and will be described in detail in the remaining chapters of this guide. Refer to Appendix Three for a detailed breakdown of each phase and its required steps.

Planning Phase.

In this initial phase, the presenter must establish the goals and objectives of the presentation based on the target audience needs and interests. He or she must analyze the target audience, define the goals or

objectives of the presentation, outline the key points that need to be made in support of the objective(s) of the presentation, and identify the location, logistics and media requirements that will support the presentation.

Design Phase. Once planning is complete, the speaker must develop the main ideas that he or she wishes to communicate to the audience using supporting data and examples.

The presenter must write a script of the presentation, and develop a strategy for handling questions from the audience. Often business presentations require review and/or approval from a superior.

If not it is still a good idea to have an informal review done by your supervisor, manager or colleague to ensure that you have not overlooked critical information.

Review is best done at the end of the design phase, before significant time has been invested in the development of the presentation and the supporting materials.

Preparation Phase.

Once the design has been completed and approved, the speaker must produce the video and audio support and handouts etc. required to support the presentation.

The presentation script is written and the supporting materials produced.

Delivery Phase. After the completion of the Preparation Phase, the speaker must now practice the presentation to master and feel comfortable delivering he information in accordance with the script, and with using the supporting materials and equipment.

On the day of the presentation, the speaker must ensure that the room is adequately equipped for the presentation. During the presentation, the speaker will circulate handouts and answer any questions

that arise (as identified in the Planning Phase).

Follow Up Phase.

The Follow-Up is a very important process that is often overlooked by most presenters. It is important to reflect back on the presentation, assessing the strong and weak points of its planning and delivery. The presenter may produce an "action item" list for questions/issues that could not be answered or resolved during the presentation. The presenter may also write summary minutes for future reference.

It is good business practice to send a thank you note to your host, particularly if you were an invited speaker. Finally, the speaker should modify the existing presentation package.

AUDIENCE ANALYSIS

For a presentation to be successful, it must be audience centred. Indeed, the characteristics of the audience significantly shape the goals and objectives of the presentation and what you, the presenter, wish to accomplish in presenting the material. By carefully analyzing your audience, and tailoring your presentation to that audience, you increase the likelihood of delivering a successful presentation and maximally prepare yourself for negative reactions and difficult questions. Consequently, everything you do in preparation must take the needs and desires of the audience into consideration.

To best serve the needs of your audience you must determine:

1. Broad demographics of your target audience (age, gender, education level, socio-economic status, position in the organization, membership in a relevant organization or special interest group, to name a few).

2. What motivated them to attend your presentation?

3. How well do they understand the subject matter?

4. What is their attitude towards you, your organization (if external) and the subject matter is?

5. How will they likely react to the presentation?

An audience analysis does not have to be a formal long drawn out process.

It can be treated as a mental exercise. If you give presentations to the same audience (i.e. your office peers and superiors) on a regular basis, you will gain more insight into their needs, expectations and background each time you present. This should make each presentation more targeted each time.

In all cases the presenter must ensure that he or she asks the right questions and determines what the impact of the collected data has on the potential goals, objectives and content of the presentation.

LOCATION, LOGISTICS AND MEDIA

You now know who your target audience is and what key points you will be presenting. You should now consider where you will be speaking, and what equipment and materials you need to ensure the success of your presentation.

Determine:

• Where will the presentation occur? Am I familiar with the room?

• Will I be presenting in the morning, afternoon, or evening?

• Does the room support my presentation? (easy to find? adequate size, temperature and lighting? flipchart? white board? tables? Podium? TV/VCR? Overhead Projector and Screen? Computer?) Do I need any additional equipment?

• Sitting or standing, will my audience members be able to see me?

• Can I just speak or do I need other equipment and/or materials to facilitate the presentation of information (flip chart & markers, Overheads, short video, handouts, whiteboard, computer, note pads

and pencils for the audience etc.)?

• Could the use of supporting materials detract from my presentation?

• What is going on in adjacent rooms? Could noise from these rooms distract the audience?

• Are there any obvious distractions? Where will late-comers enter the room (e.g., at back?)

- Where is the nearest washroom?

- Are my visual aids easy to see from different places in the room?

- How far am I from my audience? Will audience members at the back of the room be able to hear me? What are the acoustics of the room like?

KEEPING YOUR CONTENT INTERESTING

Since audience retention is lowest during the main body of the presentation, it is important to do everything you can to keep the content as interesting as possible. The following is a list of strategies that can be adopted to keep the information interesting. Note that not all strategies are appropriate for every subject matter.

- Make Comparisons. Draw comparisons between the material that you are presenting and other related but different material. This is an excellent technique to use if you are presenting technical information to non-technical people because it gives them a way of understanding your material.

- Add Humour. Depending upon the subject matter, humour is an effective tool for relaxing your audience. Once your audience is relaxed they may be more receptive to your ideas and they may retain

them longer.

Remember, humour doesn't necessarily mean telling a witty joke – you may find a cartoon, a video clip, etc. that clearly illustrates the point you are trying to make. Only use humour if you are totally comfortable in the delivery of humour and the humour is relevant to the goals and objectives and it is done in a tasteful and respective manner.

- Quote Others. This is particularly effective if the person being quoted is a well-known and respected expert in his or her field. If possible, choose quotes that are current and that are relevant to your audience (e.g., taken from a local newspaper).

• Personalize. Share your personal involvement in a subject or project with your audience. It makes the presentation more interesting and memorable to your audience.

• Support Ideas with Examples, Illustrations and Statistics. You can maintain the interest of your audience and increase your credibility as a subject matter expert by supporting your key ideas and concepts with relevant examples, illustrations and statistics. One word of caution here – use supporting materials sparingly. Since you can only present a small amount of material, you must choose the most striking ("need-to-know") information.

• Involve Your Audience. This may be accomplished by asking your audience planned questions, having them complete a worksheet or other materials, or inviting members to share relevant experiences.

Allowing your audience to be active participants in the learning process will increase their retention of the material. Audience participation must be well planned and controlled.

You may choose to use one or more of these strategies in creating your presentations. Variety, itself, will likely increase the alertness and interest level of your audience and that may positively impact on audience retention and learning.

DESIGN OF VISUAL AIDS

For a visual aid to be effective, it must be well designed. Since well-designed visual aids promote understanding, its worthwhile looking at what makes a visual aid "good". A good visual aid...

• Focuses on one important concept rather than touching upon multiple ideas, which is distracting to the viewer.

• Takes the characteristics of the audience into account. For example, a "well-designed" visual aid on a new technology will likely be very different for a technical versus a non-technical audience.

• Minimizes the use of text whenever possible. You are already speaking on the issue so why not present your supporting information in another way (e.g., graph, illustration). Just remember; only include graphics that add to what you are saying.

• Uses consistent, highly readable fonts. Stay away from fancy lettering and full capitalization (both of which are difficult to read). Also, use keywords and phrases rather than full sentences.

• Uses colours thoughtfully (i.e., to contrast or emphasize ideas or to make images more lifelike). Haphazard use of colour can result in an unattractive visual aid that detracts from the presentation.

Other characteristics will become apparent to you when you begin producing different types of presentations using a variety of media. Always keep in mind the fact that visual aids are meant to support your presentation. Visual aids should never be stand-alone. However, should the unfortunate situation arise, your presentation should be able to stand on its own, without visual support.

HANDOUTS

The purpose of a handout is to help your audience remember the information that you presented, and to remind members of how you would like them to respond to your message. The ideal handout is one well-written summary page, which outlines the key issues and resolutions discussed by the presenter. Handouts should also provide the audience with a technical or more detailed description of the materials covered in the presentation.

Handouts may also serve as a backup in the event that some or all of your visual aids are unavailable (e.g. a projector breaks down).

Handouts are intended to enhance your presentation and support your intended presentation goals and objectives. So don't include everything you know about the subject on the handout; only those points that support your intended outcomes. You should also include a list of relevant names and contact information, and anything else that the audience would have wanted to write down.

In general you should not distribute handouts before or during a presentation.

Often your audience becomes distracted and that may prevent them from hearing and processing your message. It is best to distribute handouts at the end of the presentation when you are no longer trying to maintain the audience's attention. But if your message is instructional in nature, or when

the handouts may also be used as a note taking device (such as PowerPoint handouts), or when the handout will act as an advanced organizer to guide participants through the presentation then you should distribute the handouts to all participants before the presentation and give them time to leaf through it before you begin your introduction.

You should also explain to the audience, the purpose and effective use of the handout before you begin your presentation.

DURING THE PRESENTATION: VOICE, BODY LANGUAGE & IMAGE

Your credibility as a speaker is only partly determined by what you say. How you present yourself and the material also determines how well your audience receives your message. The following tips are offered to help you deliver your presentation in the most professional and effective manner possible.

Vocal Techniques

Try to maintain a natural, conversational tone throughout your presentation.

Use language that is appropriate to your audience. If you are speaking on a topic that your audience is not familiar with, do not use jargon words or phrases and define the terminology

Try to project your voice to your entire audience. You will need to speak somewhat louder than you would during a normal conversation. You can find a volume that is comfortable for your audience when you practice in front of your "trial" audience.

To increase the dramatic effect of your presentation, you may consider varying the intensity of your speech. Varying the intensity of your speech is also an effective way to emphasize key words or concepts.

Be careful not to speak too fast or too slowly. Again, test different rates on your "trial" audience. As with intensity, varying rate can help to maintain your audience's attention and assist in creating the mood you wish to create.

Strategically placed pauses can draw attention to important points you wish to make and also helps with pausing.

A technique used by speakers to overcome filling nervous pauses with "uh", "uhm" etc. is to practice the presentation a couple of times in the following way. Each time you notice yourself saying a filler word, repeat that word several times. You will become more aware of your nervous chatter, which will help you control and eventually remove it from your speech.

Eye Contact

Establish and maintain eye contact with your audience. In doing so you communicate confidence to your audience, and will be perceived to be more credible than someone who cannot look directly at the participants. Eye contact also provides valuable feedback from you audience. (Do they look bored, confused, and/or defensive?). If you are a new presenter and you are having difficulty making eye contact with your audience, you may find one of following strategy helpful to you.

Before you begin presenting, pick a spot on the back wall (just above the audience) and present to that spot.

Over time, as you become more comfortable, pick a few friendly looking audience members, who are scattered throughout the room, and present to them.

As you gain experience and your confidence grows you will begin to look more naturally at your audience while presenting to them.

Image/Dress

Since you are giving business presentations you will want to maintain a professional image and be comfortable at the same time. Choose an outfit that is clean, neat, and comfortable, and that is appropriate for the occasion.

This does not mean that you must always wear a business suit. In fact, you may choose to wear a suit for formal presentations and to wear more casual business attire for informal gatherings. By analyzing your audience you should get a pretty good idea about how formal the meeting will be, and you can choose an outfit that is appropriate to the occasion.

Keep jewellery and other accessories to a minimum. Choose pieces that are discrete and complementary to your outfit. You don't want your attire to become the focus of your presentation. Finally, as always, ensure that you are well groomed.

Go light on any makeup and even lighter on perfumes and colognes, which some audience members may be allergic to.

Using Gestures

Gestures are a natural and common part of everyday speech. If you use gestures during your presentation, make sure that they are appropriate to the message you wish to convey to your audience. As with visual aids, they should add to your meaning, so do not use gestures for the sake of having them.

Moreover, avoid keeping your hands in motion throughout your presentation.

Such non-verbal behaviour is distracting to your audience, and reduces the meaning on any gestures that may be important to the message you are trying to convey. If you are not sure what your hands are doing while you present, videotape your next presentation (or practice session in front of "trial" audience).

You will learn a lot about your non-verbal behavior, and may discover distracting mannerisms that you never knew you had. Again, once you are aware of them, you can begin working to eliminate them.

Facial Expression

Quite simply, your facial expression should be appropriate to your message. If you are talking about a solemn or serious subject, do not try to smile throughout the presentation. It will be confusing and distracting for your audience. Try to have a varied and friendly facial expression. Most importantly, be natural and true to the tone of the subject matter.

Posture & Body Movement

As with all other non-verbal behavior, a presenter's posture and body movement can add to or detract from the message he or she is trying to communicate to the audience.

Avoid the following behaviors, which are distracting to your audience.

If you use a podium, do not rock it back and forth or grip the sides of it. You will appear nervous and possibly even defensive.

Don't sway or pace around the room. Again, you will seem nervous and your unnatural movement will distract the audience.

If you feel more comfortable standing, stand straight, with your feet a comfortable distance apart. Bend your knees slightly and distribute most of your weight to the balls of your feet. If you prefer to move (from time to time) around the room, take the necessary steps to move to your new position and then return to your comfortable standing position.

There is advantage to moving occasionally around the room. It can help you to connect with your audience and to maintain your audience's attention and interest. You may also find that occasional movement helps you to become more relaxed.

Movement can also help you to change the mood or pace of the presentation.

With respect to posture, if you are standing, stand up straight and hold your head up. The recommendations are the same if you are sitting – sit up straight and hold your head up. Also, if you are sitting, ensure that all audience members can clearly see you. Adopt an open posture. Do not cross your arms in front of you (which is usually seen as a defensive stance) but rather let your arms hang comfortably by your side when you are not gesturing to your audience.

Handling Nervousness

Even the most experienced presenters experience nervousness from time to time. Common signs of nervousness include having a dry mouth or tight throat, shaking, perspiring and/or having "butterflies" in your stomach.

Nervousness often stems from a feeling of being unprepared, so ensure that you are well prepared and practiced prior to the day of the presentation. Also, take the time to prepare answers to questions you are likely to be asked, and prepare supporting overheads for any difficult questions.

In doing this, you will go into your presentation knowing that you are maximally prepared.

Some experts suggest that you complete the following visualization exercise to reduce nervousness. Visualize yourself as a confident and competent presenter giving a successful presentation. This will help you to focus on your positive attributes and on the strengths of your presentation.

Before the presentation eat lightly and avoid caffeine.

Arrive at the venue early so that you can become familiar and comfortable with the room and to

check that all equipment is available and working. You may even want to memorize the opening remarks of your presentation and warm up for the presentation by practicing the introduction a couple of times before the audience arrives. Another reason you may wish to memorize your opening statements is that for most presenters, the first few minutes are the hardest.

Getting off to a smooth start can be a huge confidence builder.

Before you begin your presentation, take a moment to concentrate on your breathing. When we are nervous, our breathing tends to become shallow – to combat this practice taking slow, deep breaths. The air should fill your diaphragm. This usually results in a reduction in the feeling of nervousness.

Remember to breathe throughout your presentation. Also, make sure that you have a glass of water available (you may have to bring your own) so that if you experience a dry mouth or throat, you can pause, take a quick drink, and then continue with your presentation. And if you experience voice shakiness try lowering the pitch or increasing the volume of your voice.

Again, pre-presentation nervousness is very common. When you experience it remember that you are not alone. Remind yourself that you are well prepared and that you are ready to present to your audience. Use the techniques above to turn the nervousness into beneficial rather than detrimental energy.

Answering Questions…when?

Whether it is best to answer questions during or after your presentation is a difficult question to answer.

Some experts advise against answering questions during the presentation because it breaks the flow of the presentations and often the questions being asked anticipate topics that will be covered later. Since you have spent considerable time preparing to speak, you want to ensure that you deliver your entire message.

In contrast, some experts recommend that you answer questions as they come up rather than waiting until the end. These experts reason that the answers to the questions will be more meaningful to the audience as a whole if given while the topic is being covered. If you choose to answer questions throughout your presentation, make sure that you schedule some time for question and answer time for each topic and stick to your schedule.

That way you will be able to answer most questions without losing the flow of the presentation.

A second option is to answer all questions at the end of your presentation.

This way you will ensure that you cover all the material without interruption.

A disadvantage to choosing this approach is that your audience may remember more about the particular questions asked than about the summary of your presentation (because audience members tend to remember the beginnings and endings of presentations best and you have ended your presentation with a question and answer period). This could be detrimental to the overall success of the presentation if you have trouble answering any questions or dealing with difficult audience members.

An alternative approach is to schedule a question and answer session prior to your presentation summary. This way you will insure that you cover all the required material, deal with any questions that arise, and end the presentation on a strong note, by summarizing your key points. If you have any difficulty during the question and answer session, you have an opportunity to re-establish your credibility and re-state your ideas during your final summary.

General Rules for Answering Questions:

Here are some general rules for responding to inquiries from your audience:

• Be positive and open to questions. You are an expert in your subject matter and have spent time preparing answers to potential audience questions. Approach this part of the presentation as an opportunity to further state and clarify your message.

• Before you respond, ensure that you understand the question. You can do this by repeating or paraphrasing the question. In doing so, you will ensure that all audience members have heard and understood the question.

• Remain focused. Respond to the question in terms of its relevance to your presentation goal. To do this you might follow a procedure similar to that used to prepare for impromptu speeches.

• Prepare overheads (or other supporting materials) for difficult questions a head of time. Your audience will be impressed by your preplanning and preparations.

Handling Difficult Questions and/or Audience Members

From time to time you will be faced with a question that is too difficult or time consuming to answer or that somehow diverts you from the goals and objectives of your presentation. Here are some strategies for handling difficult questions and/or difficult audience members.

If you are unable to answer a question be straightforward about it with your audience and offer to follow up with an answer to the question in writing.

Then make it your top post-presentation priority to provide your audience members with the answer to the question. Never try to ""bluff" your way through a question – the audience can usually tell and it will not leave a favorable impression.

If someone asks a question that is diversionary or that is about a subject that will be discussed later, answer the question briefly and/or indicate that the subject will be dealt with later in the presentation and then refocus the audience back to the original topic and continue.

If someone asks you a series of vaguely related questions or has trouble getting to the point, you must tactfully "step in" and help the questioner focus his or her question to a key issue. You might approach this as if you were paraphrasing the person's question – e.g., "If I understand you correctly, you are looking for clarification on…"

If you encounter an argumentative audience member, acknowledge the person's concern by stating that his/her point deserves further analysis, offer to follow up with that person on the issue at a later date, and then refocus your audience back to the original topic and continue.

Always be diplomatic and never argue with your audience member. Arguing is a waste of time, and

if you make an audience member look foolish or wrong you risk making an unfavourable impression on the rest of the audience.

An effective strategy to use if you are asked a question that cannot be answered or that is designed to put you on the defensive is to reflect the question back to the questioner. Another option is to put the question on the floor for all audience members to comment on.

Recognize that with this type of question, the questioner has anticipated your answer and is ready with a reply to contradict your response. Don't play the game. Acknowledge that the issue is important to that individual, offer to discuss it further at a later time, refocus your audience back to the original topic, and then continue.

Remember that in most cases, audience members will be friendly and questions will be straightforward. Let your audience know that you welcome their questions and feedback. Ensure that your audience clearly understands the goals of your presentation and what actions you would like from them after the presentation.

SUMMARY

The ability to deliver effective presentations is a key competency for all business professionals. You must be able to communicate your message to an audience. You must be able to influence that audience to act in the way that you would like them to. To do so you must think about your audience, you must design a visually effective presentation and you must learn to deliver it in a confident and professional manner.

ASSIGNMENT

The final assignment for this unit requires that you produce and deliver a formal presentation to an audience of your choice. You will be required to submit a copy of your PowerPoint presentation and a video tape of your presentation to your instructor for review, feedback and grading.

Instructions

Select an audience that you are familiar with. Offer to provide a formal presentation about your business idea or a topic that you have expertise in.

Produce an appropriate 20 to 30 minute presentation. Identify an appropriate location to deliver the presentation and provide an appropriate handout for the audience.

Once you have completed your presentation solicit verbal feedback from your peers.

Produce a two or three page report based on the feedback from the audience.

BIBLIOGRAPHY/REFERENCES

• Suite101.com. (2008). Elements of the Communications Process.

(Online Article). Available at:

http://valerielizotte.suite101.com/communication-modela58125#ixzz1JMdta2yk

*the Commonwealth of Learning CC-BY-SA (share alike with attribution).http://creativecommons.org/licenses/by-sa/4.0

• MindTools.com. (nd.). Why Communications Skills are So Important.

(Online Article). Available at:

http://www.mindtools.com/CommSkll/Communication-Intro.htm

• ArticleBase.com. (2009). (Web Site). Types of Communication and Its

Characteristics. Available at: http://www.articlesbase.com/selfPage

improvement-articles/types-of-communication-and-its-characteristics-872799.html

• Buzzle.com. (nd.). Types of Communications. (Web Site). Available at: http://www.buzzle.com/articles/types-of-communication.html

• Mindtools.com. (nd.). How Good Are Your Communication Skills?

(Online Quiz). Available at:

http://www.mindtools.com/pages/article/newCS_99.htm

• Buzzle.com. (nd.). List of Communications Skills. (Online Article).

Available at: http://www.buzzle.com/articles/list-of-communicationskills.html

• Buzzle.com. (nd.). Type of Non-Verbal Communications. (Online Article). Available at: http://www.buzzle.com/articles/types-ofnonverbal-communication.html

• ManagementStudyGuide.com. (nd.). Overcoming Communications Barriers. (Web Site). Available at:

http://www.managementstudyguide.com/overcomingcommunication-barriers.htm

• SkillsYouNeed.co.uk. (nd.) Interpersonal Communications Skills.(Web Site). Available at:

http://www.skillsyouneed.co.uk/IPS/Interpersonal_Communication.html

D.K.Berlo. (1960). The Process of Communication. New York: Holt, Rinehart and Winston.

Taylor, S. (1999). In Communication for Business. Pearsons Education Inc, New York.

William J. Seiler, M. L. (2002). In Communication- Making Connections. Boston: Pearsons Education.

Zeuschner, R. (2003). In Communications Today - The Essentials. boston: Pearsons Education Inc.

Business Communications- Virtual University of Pakistan

Communication Module in VUSCC – Tour guide course material

Non Verbal Communication. (n.d.). Retrieved march 17, 2011, from

www.buzzle.com: http://www.buzzle.com/articles/types-of-nonverbalcommunication.html

Overcoming Communication Barriers. (n.d.). Retrieved March 18, 2011, from

www.managementstudyguide.com:

http://www.managementstudyguide.com/overcoming-communicationbarriers.

DISCLAIMER

Disclaimer All the material contained in this book is provided for educational and informational purposes only. No responsibility can be taken for any results or outcomes resulting from the use of this material. While every attempt has been made to provide information that is both accurate and effective, the author does not assume any responsibility for the accuracy or use/misuse of this information.

www.ingramcontent.com/pod-product-compliance
Lightning Source LLC
Chambersburg PA
CBHW021814170526
45157CB00007B/2587